DRIP-FREE MARRIAGE

How to Stop the Slow Leaks That Ruin Love

Dr. Elsworth Neale, PhD

ISBN: 979-8-9937201-4-2

Printed in the United States of America

Dedication

***

This book is dedicated to my mother and father, who were married for forty years and departed this life only two weeks apart, their covenant having taught them how to live together, and how not to remain when one was gone.

It is also dedicated to my wife, my covenant companion, with whom I share the daily joy of building, honoring, and sustaining a love worth keeping.

And to marriages everywhere, may they be guarded with wisdom, restored with grace, and strengthened over time to become shelter, witness, and blessing for generations to come.

Foreword

***

Marriage today is often treated as disposable, optional, or outdated. Yet Scripture presents marriage as a sacred, formative, and enduring covenant. In *Drip-Free Marriage*, Dr. Elsworth Neale offers a timely and necessary contribution to this conversation.

This book does not approach marriage as an ideal to admire from a distance, nor as a problem to manage with techniques alone. Instead, it frames marriage as a living structure, one that must be inspected, maintained, repaired, and sealed over time. The metaphor of *"drips"* is both practical and prophetic. It reminds us that most marriages do not collapse suddenly; they erode quietly.

What I appreciate most about this work is its balance. Dr. Neale integrates biblical theology, relational psychology, pastoral wisdom, and lived experience with clarity and compassion. He does not shame struggling couples, nor does he romanticize endurance. Instead, he invites couples into the holy work of maintenance, where grace meets responsibility, and love learns how to stay.

Whether you are newly married, decades into covenant, or preparing for marriage, this book will challenge you to listen for the drips, seal the leaks, and build a marriage that becomes shelter for generations.

I commend this book to you with confidence and prayer.

Dr. Peter Bonadie

Senior Pastor, Kingdom Life Ministries International

Founder, Peter Bonadie Worldwide

Preface

***

I did not write this book because I believe marriage is easy. I wrote it because marriage is worth keeping.

Over years of counseling, teaching, research, and walking alongside couples, I've learned that most marriages do not fail from lack of love, faith, or intention. They fail due to unattended leaks. The small, ordinary places where tenderness dries up, communication erodes, and connection quietly escapes.

This book is not a manual, a sermon, or a list of rules. It is an invitation to see marriage clearly, to tend it wisely, and to believe that restoration is always possible. Whether you are repairing damage or strengthening what already stands, I hope that these pages help you build a marriage that does not merely survive storms but becomes shelter in them.

Contents

SECTION II — THE OILS & SEALANTS THAT KEEP LOVE ALIVE

THE DRIP CYCLE™

How disconnection happens

Small moments → Repeated patterns → Relationship breakdown

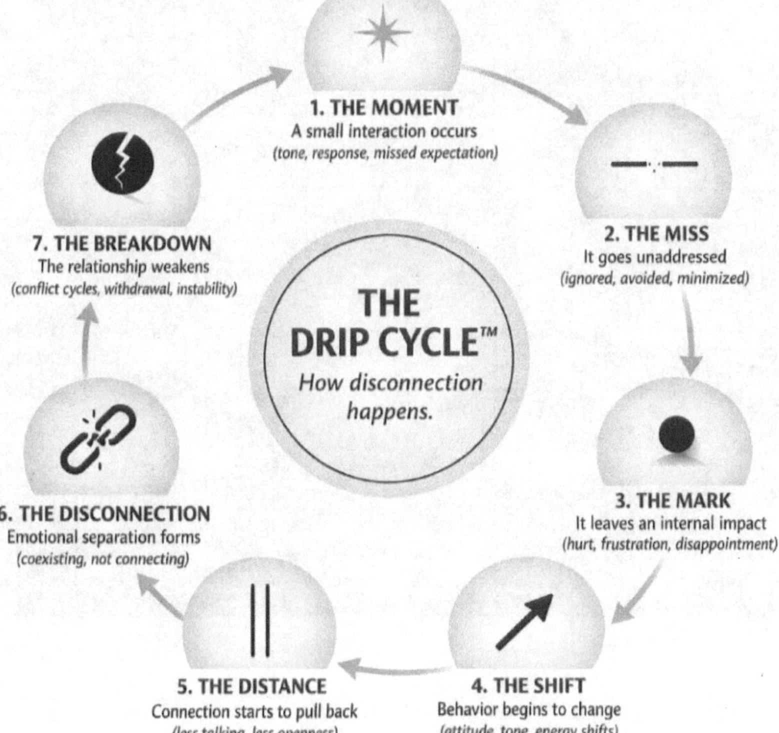

Most marriages don't have a major problem—
they are stuck in a cycle.

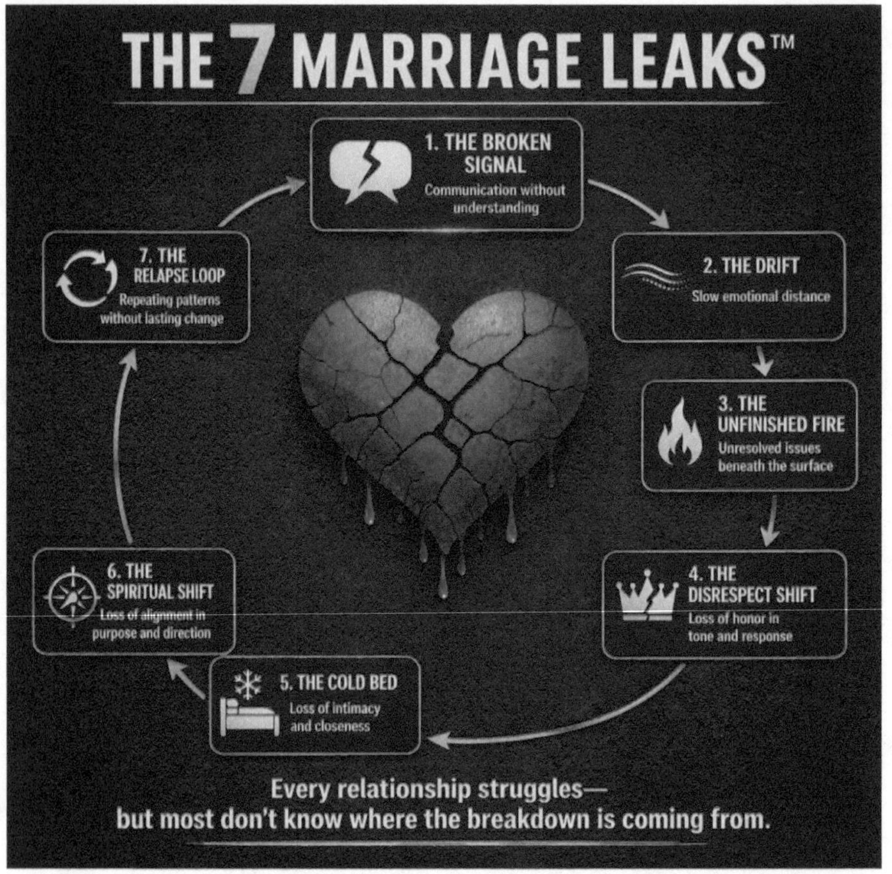
THE 7 MARRIAGE LEAKS™
1. THE BROKEN SIGNAL
Communication without understanding
2. THE DRIFT
Slow emotional distance
3. THE UNFINISHED FIRE
Unresolved issues beneath the surface
4. THE DISRESPECT SHIFT
Loss of honor in tone and response
5. THE COLD BED
Loss of intimacy and closeness
6. THE SPIRITUAL SHIFT
Loss of alignment in purpose and direction
7. THE RELAPSE LOOP
Repeating patterns without lasting change
Every relationship struggles—
but most don't know where the breakdown is coming from.

Understanding Your Marriage Through The System

Before we go further, take a moment to reflect:

• Where are you in the cycle?

• Which leak shows up most in your relationship?

You may not see everything clearly yet—and that's okay. As you continue through this book, you will begin to recognize patterns, identify the leaks, and understand how small moments have shaped your relationship over time.

This is not about blame.

It's about awareness.

And awareness is where repair begins.

Introduction

Why Marriages Drip (And Why They Don't Have To)

***

Most marriages don't collapse all at once. They erode.

When people imagine a relationship falling apart, they often picture dramatic explosions, betrayal, abandonment, or crisis-level conflict. And yes, some marriages do end with those kinds of storms. But more often, love is not lost through catastrophe. It leaks away slowly.

If you've ever lived in a house with a leaky faucet or roof, you know how quiet the danger can be. At first, the drip is just background noise, barely noticeable, almost harmless. But left long enough, it becomes maddening. Worse still, the real damage is not what you hear; it's what's happening behind the walls. Water seeps into joists, weakens beams, and feeds mold. A gentle drip can ruin an entire structure.

Marriage suffers the same way. Most couples don't fragment because of a single event. They leak through silence, neglect, unresolved conflict, sarcasm, bitterness, unspoken disappointment, or the quiet drift of two people who stop paying attention.

One unaddressed irritation at dinner. One night of scrolling instead of talking. One week without affection. One month without intimacy. One year without true conversation. By the time cracks are visible, the erosion has been spreading quietly for years.

The Bible captures this dynamic with surprising clarity:

"A quarrelsome wife is like the dripping of a leaky roof in a rainstorm" (Proverbs 27:15, NIV).

The Message paraphrases it vividly:

"A nagging spouse is like the drip, drip, drip of a leaky faucet."

The imagery is unforgettable. A constant drip doesn't just irritate; it wears down the soul. And while the proverb highlights one type of leak, the principle extends further.

A marriage can leak from pornography, emotional affairs, chronic criticism, passive withdrawal, contempt, or secrets that never come into the light.

This book is about those drips; naming them, noticing them, and by God's grace, stopping them before love runs dry. Most couples never intend for their marriages to grow cold. Just as no homeowner plans to let the roof rot, no spouse wakes up and thinks, "I'd like to slowly destroy the affection in my home." But leaks don't require malice. They require inattention.

Ecclesiastes 10:18 warns us:

"Through laziness, the rafters sag; because of idle hands, the house leaks" (NIV).

Marriages sag for the same reasons, not always through intentional harm, but through neglect. What is not maintained eventually collapses.

Erosion looks ordinary. A husband pours his passion into work and arrives home with nothing left for his wife. A wife swallows her disappointment until it seeps out in sarcasm. Days go by without laughter. Weeks go by without touch. Arguments simmer beneath polite silence. Intimacy becomes mechanical or disappears altogether. Affection evaporates. Respect thins. The marriage still has walls, but there is no warmth in the rooms.

Here's the hope: the God who designed the covenant did not design it to be fragile.

Isaiah 58:12 describes Him as the One who empowers His people to *"raise up the foundations of many generations"* and be called *"The Repairer of the Breach, the Restorer of Streets to Dwell In" (AMP).*

That restoration includes marriages. Leaks can be found. Cracks can be sealed. Foundations can be strengthened. Homes can be made safe again.

To pursue a drip-free marriage does not mean your relationship will never face storms. It means you will learn how to repair quickly, maintain intentionally, and build with wisdom so the storms do not sweep the house away.

If you feel the weight of leaks in your relationship as you read this, take heart. This is not a book about blame or humiliation. It is not written to make one spouse the problem and the other the victim. It is written to invite both into restoration.

And if your marriage currently feels strong, don't skip ahead assuming this book isn't for you. A wise couple doesn't wait until the ceiling caves in to check the roof. Prevention is as holy as repair.

Why "Drip-Free"?

The problem in marriage is not water. Water sustains life. The problem is water escaping its boundaries.

A drip-free home is not a home with no water; it is a home where water flows where it is meant to and nowhere else.

The same is true of love. Desire, conflict, passion, anger, affection—these are not the enemies of marriage. They are part of its flow.

The danger begins when communication leaks into criticism, when desire leaks into pornography, when energy leaks into another relationship, when time leaks into distraction instead of connection. That is how love runs dry. A drip-free marriage is not a perfect marriage. It is a maintained marriage. A repaired marriage. A sealed and tended marriage. A covenant where joy, intimacy, respect, and tenderness can flow freely without escaping through the cracks.

Marriage was God's idea long before it was ours. In Genesis, we read:

"That is why a man leaves his father and mother and is united to his wife, and they become one flesh" (Gen. 2:24, NIV).

Paul later anchors this in Christ's love for the church:

"For husbands, this means love your wives, just as Christ loved the church" (Eph. 5:25, NLT).

This is not sentimental language. It is sacrificial, restorative, and covenantal.

Scripture never treats marriage as disposable. It treats it as shelter. As a garden. As a fountain. As witness. As legacy. *Song of Solomon* describes it as

"A garden fountain, a well of fresh water" (Song 4:15, NLT).

God does not intend the covenant to drip. He intends it to overflow.

We live in a cultural moment where marriage is both idealized and neglected. Social media fuels comparison. Pornography shapes distorted expectations. Busyness replaces intimacy. Careers displace connection. Even in the church, couples often drown quietly, afraid to admit they are leaking.

But strong marriages matter, not only for personal happiness, but for witness and legacy. A marriage that holds becomes a shelter for more than just the couple inside it. It shelters children, grandchildren, spiritual sons and daughters, and entire communities.

When marriages thrive, families strengthen. When families strengthen, communities heal.

A Word Before We Begin

Whether your marriage is in crisis, in maintenance, or in celebration, this book is for you. Every covenant carries leaks somewhere. Every home needs inspection. Every couple needs repair. The good news is that nothing you will face catches God unprepared. With Him as the third strand,

"A cord of three strands is not quickly broken" (Ecclesiastes 4:12, NIV).

Your marriage is too precious to let it drip away. Together, we'll learn how to seal the cracks, restore what has weakened, and strengthen what remains.

Let's begin the journey toward a marriage that doesn't merely survive but holds.

Chapter 1

Your Marriage Is One of a Kind

***

Every marriage begins with a story, and no two stories are alike. Some start like fairy tales, with sparks flying from the first encounter. Others begin quietly, two coworkers sharing coffee breaks, or childhood friends who slowly realize friendship has deepened into something far stronger. Still others emerge from second chances after heartbreak or loss, blending families or discovering love later in life when it seemed unlikely.

Each story is unique because the people in it are unique. And when two unique people form a covenant, they create something that has never existed before and will never exist again. Your marriage is not a replica. It is a one-of-a-kind design, shaped by unrepeatable personalities, histories, and callings. While society loves patterns and comparisons, a covenant is always personal. God does not mass-produce marriages; He handcrafts covenants.

Yet modern culture makes it easy to forget this. We live in an age where comparison is constant and often subconscious.

You scroll through your phone and see curated images of couples on tropical vacations, renewing their vows on breathtaking beaches, enjoying anniversary dinners under string lights, posing in matching outfits, or posting tributes full of poetic language. It's easy to wonder: Why don't we look like that quietly? Why aren't we doing those things? Why doesn't our marriage feel like their marriage seems to feel?

Comparison rarely shows up as a crisis. It shows up as a slow drip, subtle and unannounced. Drips don't demand attention. They don't alarm you like a burst pipe. Instead, they whisper: Look at them. Look at what you don't have. Look at what you're not doing. Look at how far behind you are. Over time, that drip begins to shape how couples interpret their own marriage. Instead of valuing the covenant they actually have, they begin to resent the one they don't.

Couples don't compare because they are shallow. They compare because they are human. People interpret their lives through reference points; what they see, hear, and experience in others. The danger emerges when those reference points become measurements of worth.

Suddenly, what was once gratitude becomes dissatisfaction. What was once normal becomes *"not enough."*

In coaching and counseling environments, I often hear statements like:

- "We're behind."
- "We don't communicate as they do."
- "Other couples pray together more than we do."
- "We should be further along by now."
- "Other people's marriages seem happier than ours."

These are not statements of curiosity; they are statements of judgment. Judgment creates pressure. And pressure rarely brings couples closer; it often strains them.

The apostle Paul warned the early church about the dangers of self-measurement. He wrote:

"When they measure themselves by themselves and compare themselves with themselves, they are not wise." (2 Corinthians 10:12, NIV)

Comparison is unwise not only because it distorts reality but because it distracts from stewardship.

When you are busy measuring your marriage against someone else's, you are not nurturing your own covenant. You are auditing it.

Social media intensifies this because it allows people to display edited highlights without revealing context. You may see a couple posting smiling anniversary photos, but not the argument they had the night before. You may see glamorous vacation pictures, but not the credit card debt that financed them. You may see extravagant date nights, but not the childcare exhaustion of that same week. You may see consistent ministry partnership, but not the private counseling sessions and boundaries that kept that partnership healthy.

Every couple has battles the outside world will never see. That's why comparing your unfiltered reality to someone else's curated image is a guaranteed way to feel inadequate. It's like judging a construction site against a finished home; one will always look messier.

The truth is that every marriage has both beautiful and difficult seasons. Newlyweds may wrestle with merging expectations and family cultures. Couples raising young children may struggle to maintain connection and energy. Blended families may navigate complex loyalties and rhythms. Empty nesters may rediscover identity after decades of parenting.

Each season brings both grace and challenge. None of these seasons is a failure; each is part of the story.

But comparison blinds couples to the beauty of their own season. Instead of asking, "What is God building in us right now?" couples ask, "Why don't we look like them?" That shift steals joy and breeds resentment. The slow drip of comparison becomes a leak in the roof of covenant, weakening beams that were once strong.

Andre and Keisha (names changed for discretion) illustrate this well. Their marriage wasn't broken. They loved each other. They shared values. They hadn't experienced infidelity, abuse, or abandonment. What they experienced was quieter: discontent. Keisha watched videos and photos of couples who seemed to be living more exciting lives, traveling, renovating homes, attending events, and taking glamorous photos. Andre compared himself financially to friends who seemed to be *"further along."* They were not angry; they were tired. Not disconnected; just discouraged. Nothing dramatic happened, yet something meaningful was eroding.

What eroded wasn't love; it was uniqueness. The sense that our marriage is allowed to be ours.

Your covenant is not required to match the personality, ministry, finances, or social rhythms of anybody else's. Some couples thrive on adventure and travel; others thrive on peace and routine. Some love hosting people constantly; others serve in quieter, less visible ways.

Some are affectionate in public; others are deeply bonded in private. None of these differences determines spiritual maturity or marital quality.

One of the most damaging assumptions couples make is that there is a singular way to be "successful" in marriage. There isn't. Marriage is not standardized. It is contextual. The expressions of love, connection, intimacy, and partnership will always reflect the wiring of the two people involved.

This is why the Bible uses the language of covenant rather than competition. Covenant assumes uniqueness. God told Adam:

"It is not good for the man to be alone; I will make a helper suitable for him." (Genesis 2:18, NIV)

The word *suitable* does not mean identical. It means corresponding, complementary, and appropriately matched for the assignment and design of the two involved. When Scripture later declares:

"...and they shall become one flesh." (Genesis 2:24, NIV)

It is describing a process, not an immediate reality. Oneness is not microwaved. It is cultivated.

Becoming one flesh requires that the two people involved honor their distinctiveness while learning to harmonize their lives. Harmonizing is not the same as cloning. In music, harmony requires different notes, not identical ones. Marriage works the same way. Differences are not the enemy of covenant; they are raw materials for unity.

But unity cannot flourish where comparison dominates. Comparison leads to imitation, and imitation suffocates authenticity. When couples imitate the marriages they admire, copying their habits, their ministry patterns, their personalities, or their romantic expressions, they often lose sight of what God is actually asking them to build. Imitation may look admirable from the outside, but it feels burdensome on the inside because it requires becoming someone other than yourself.

Uniqueness is not just a poetic idea; it is a protective factor. Couples who understand their uniqueness are less threatened by outside expectations, less likely to resent one another's differences, and less likely to mistake someone else's calling for their own. They are also less likely to pressure each other into roles that don't fit.

The measure of your marriage is not how much it resembles someone else's, but how faithfully you steward the covenant entrusted to you.

If marriage is one of a kind, then it also carries a one-of-a-kind assignment. Scripture never presents marriage as merely a romantic partnership or shared life logistics. It presents marriage as a covenant, with the purpose of two stories becoming one for the sake of something bigger than either could accomplish alone. From the beginning, marriage is connected to calling. In Genesis, we read:

"Then God blessed them, and God said to them, 'Be fruitful and multiply; fill the earth and subdue it...'" (Genesis 1:28, NKJV)

Before there was a wedding ceremony, before there were children, before there was community, there was assignment. God blessed the union and then gave it purpose. Fruitfulness in Scripture is never limited to biology. It includes productivity, creativity, influence, stewardship, and contribution to the world around us. Marriage was designed not simply for companionship, but for co-labor.

This means your marriage has work to do, not necessarily work that looks like public ministry or platform visibility, but work that reflects Heaven's priorities through your shared life. For some couples, that assignment may be visible.

For others, it may be hidden. For many, it may change across seasons. But the point remains: covenant is never purposeless.

When couples do not understand or acknowledge their assignment, they drift toward imitation.

They begin to adopt patterns, values, and rhythms from the marriages they admire rather than discerning the marriage they were entrusted with. Imitation feels safe because it provides a template, but it rarely fits. Templates can be helpful for inspiration, but they cannot replace discernment. No two marriages are given the same geography, resources, temperaments, histories, or wounds. Therefore, no two marriages can be expected to fulfill the same assignment in the same way.

God equips marriages differently because He calls them differently. The apostle Paul wrote:

"Each one should test their own actions. Then they can take pride in themselves alone, without comparing themselves to someone else..." (Galatians 6:4, NIV)

Testing your own actions means evaluating your covenant in light of your calling, not somebody else's. Pride here is not arrogance; it is satisfaction in faithful stewardship.

When couples evaluate themselves according to foreign assignments, they inevitably conclude they are failing. Some couples are called to build a spiritual legacy through discipleship and mentorship. Others are called to adopt children or care for aging parents. Others are called to build businesses, or create spaces of hospitality, or steward financial resources, or champion justice, or anchor stability within their communities. None of these assignments is more spiritual than the others. All of them can be expressions of covenant purpose.

The assignment also explains why some marriages experience more warfare than others. The enemy rarely opposes what is meaningless. He opposes what is fruitful. Many couples assume their struggles are signs of incompatibility when they may, in fact, be signs of assignment. When you carry spiritual responsibility together, you will experience spiritual resistance together. That resistance is not evidence that your marriage is failing; it may be evidence that it matters.

Understanding assignment requires couples to stop asking, "What do other marriages look like?" and start asking, "What have we been called to build together?" That question shifts the focus from performance to purpose. Purpose brings alignment.

Alignment produces unity. Unity generates authority. Unity is not created by sameness; it is created by agreement.

Amos asks:

"Can two walk together, unless they are agreed?" (Amos 3:3, NKJV)

An agreement does not mean the absence of difference. It means shared direction. Many marriages are full of love but lack agreement. They are emotionally connected but strategically scattered. Without shared direction, marriages drift into frustration. With shared direction, marriages develop momentum.

Momentum may not always look exciting. Sometimes momentum looks like consistency showing up for work, raising children, paying bills, caring for relatives, and stewarding health. The beauty of a covenant is found not only in milestones but in maintenance. Maintenance is not evidence of stagnation; it is evidence of stewardship. A marriage that practices maintenance will outlast a marriage addicted to novelty. The danger is that maintenance is rarely celebrated publicly. No one posts pictures of paying off debt, cooking dinner, honoring boundaries, or setting healthy rhythms. But these are the quiet practices that make a covenant durable.

A marriage with assignment cannot afford to despise the ordinary. Ordinary faithfulness is the soil in which extraordinary fruitfulness grows.

Andre and Keisha struggled in this area. They admired couples who traveled frequently and posted ministry updates online. They saw other couples hosting gatherings and leading small groups.

They saw friends renovating homes and celebrating milestones. Meanwhile, they were in a season of financial reconstruction and internal healing. Their assignment was not visibility; it was stabilization. They needed to rebuild trust with finances, with scheduling, and with communication. That season didn't look glamorous. It looked like budgeting, going to bed earlier, saying no to unnecessary commitments, and reducing noise. None of that was social media worthy, but it was covenant-worthy.

Assignments also evolve. The assignment of a marriage with toddlers will not resemble the assignment of a marriage with teenagers, empty nesters, or retirees. Every season prepares the next. The worst thing a couple can do is romanticize a season they are not in or resent a season they are required to pass through. Resentment of the season is one of the quietest ways comparisons drain joy.

The psalmist writes:

"He makes everything beautiful in its time." (Ecclesiastes 3:11, NIV)

Beauty is seasonal. Fruit is seasonal. Assignment is seasonal. You cannot reap in winter, and you cannot sow in harvest. Marriage requires discernment of timing. When couples embrace seasonality, they stop competing with other people's timelines.

Purpose also reframes difference. In many marriages, the traits that frustrate initially are the traits that prove essential to the assignment. A visionary spouse may seem unrealistic until vision is needed to step into new territory. A detail-oriented spouse may seem controlling until precision is required to execute plans. A relational spouse may seem overly social until relationships open doors. God often matches assignments to temperament.

These differences are not random. They are design features. Each spouse brings grace. Grace in Scripture is not just unmerited favor; it is operational empowerment. The apostle Peter wrote:

"Each one should use whatever gift he has received to serve others..." (1 Peter 4:10, NIV)

Marriage multiplies grace by combining gifts. One spouse may carry administrative grace; another may carry relational grace.

One may carry financial grace, another emotional grace. One may bring creativity, another stability. Covenant is the joining of graces for the fulfillment of an assignment.

The assignment also explains why certain couples attract certain people. Some attract the broken, others attract leaders, others attract children or young adults, others attract entrepreneurs, others attract families, and others attract no one for a season because they are being formed internally.

This is not a coincidence. It is the alignment between grace and need. The people drawn to your marriage often reveal who you are called to serve.

When couples understand their assignment, comparison loses its power. You cannot envy a race you are not running. You cannot resent seeds you were not called to plant. You cannot covet fruit that does not belong to your field. The question becomes not, "Are we like them?" but *"Are we faithful to what has been entrusted to us?"*

Covenant is not performance. It is stewardship. God does not ask couples to impress Him with their marriage. He asks them to partner with Him in their marriage. That partnership is activated through agreement, sustained through maintenance, and tested through seasons.

Every assignment has costs. Some assignments cost privacy, others cost time, others cost finances, others cost comfort, and others cost reputation. But assignments also carry reward, meaning, fruitfulness, legacy, and testimony.

Legacy is not merely what you leave for people. Legacy is what you leave in people. A covenant lived on purpose leaves something in the world that would not exist without it.

If your marriage is one of a kind and carries a unique assignment, then it must also be protected.

Not all pressure is external, and not all threats are dramatic. Many marriages are not destroyed by explosions but weakened by small, persistent leaks that go unaddressed. Couples expect crisis to come loudly, but crisis often comes quietly. Protecting the uniqueness of your covenant requires intentional boundaries, thoughtful stewardship, and courage to resist the templates and expectations of others.

Boundaries are not walls; they are doors. Walls keep everything out. Doors allow the right things in and keep the wrong things out. In marriage, boundaries protect covenants from intrusion, comparison, overcommitment, and competing voices.

Some boundaries are interpersonal, others are familial, and others are cultural or even internal.

One of the most overlooked boundaries in marriage is the boundary against unnecessary comparison. Comparison is not only social; it can be familial. Couples often inherit expectations about what marriage should look like from parents, siblings, relatives, or the cultural community. Sometimes these expectations are helpful; often they are burdensome.

A couple may feel pressure to have children by a certain age, to buy a home quickly, to earn a certain income, to join certain ministries, to show affection publicly, or to match the lifestyle of peers.

But none of these pressures considers season, assignment, personality, or grace. Pressure without discernment produces resentment, and resentment erodes connection.

Another boundary is time. Many marriages fail not because of a lack of love, but because of a lack of availability. Love without time feels like neglect. Intentional availability requires boundaries around work, ministry, technology, and other commitments. Many couples give the best of their energy to everything except each other, assuming the marriage will absorb whatever remains.

But Covenant Health cannot survive on leftovers. Marriage needs priority, and priority is revealed not by words but by allocation of time and attention.

Protecting uniqueness also requires reframing the ordinary. Modern culture glamorizes novelty and visibility, but most of covenant life is quiet and unseen. Paying bills, preparing meals, cleaning homes, folding laundry, commuting to work, meeting extended family obligations, attending children's events, and navigating illness or loss; these do not appear extraordinary from the outside, yet they are the rhythms that build intimacy and trust.

Jesus Himself spent most of His earthly life in obscurity working, honoring His parents, learning, and simply inhabiting His calling.

Scripture records:

"...Jesus grew in wisdom and in stature and in favor with God and all the people." (Luke 2:52, NLT)

Growth happened quietly before ministry happened publicly. Marriage works the same way. The ordinary is not second-class; it is foundational. Couples who learn to honor the ordinary often experience greater stability and less disappointment. *Ordinary faithfulness* is often the greatest testimony a marriage can give.

Andre and Keisha eventually discovered this. After wrestling with comparison, they realized their covenant was entering a formation season, not a showcase season. Their calling at that time was to stabilize, not to impress. Once they embraced this, the pressure to imitate others was released. They stopped resenting their pace and began stewarding their season. Peace returned, not because circumstances changed, but because perspective did.

Protecting uniqueness also requires guarding the voices that have access to your covenant. Not every voice should be granted influence. Well-meaning family and friends can unintentionally impose their values, fears, or expectations on a marriage.

Couples must discern between advice that aligns with their assignment and advice that distracts from it.

The apostle Paul declared:

"All things are lawful for me, but not all things are beneficial..." (1 Corinthians 10:23, AMP)

Marriage demands the same wisdom: not everything is beneficial for your covenant. Some activities are neutral for others but destabilizing for you. Some commitments are life-giving for another couple but draining for yours. Protecting uniqueness requires permission to say no, even to good things.

Spiritual protection matters as well. Marriage invites spiritual warfare because a covenant reflects God's design for unity, generational influence, and fruitfulness. Jesus taught:

"Every kingdom divided against itself is headed for destruction, and no house divided against itself will stand." (Matthew 12:25, CSB)

Division is one of the enemy's oldest strategies. Division may not always appear as conflict. Sometimes it appears as a distraction, discouragement, or comparison. The enemy rarely needs to destroy a marriage if he can distract it from its assignment. A distracted marriage is a neutralized marriage.

Protection finally requires gentleness. In our era, gentleness is often mistaken for weakness, but gentleness is strength under control.

The apostle Paul urged:

"Be completely humble and gentle; be patient, bearing with one another in love." (Ephesians 4:2, NIV)

Gentleness creates safety. Safety produces vulnerability. Vulnerability produces intimacy. Intimacy sustains covenant. Many marriages do not lack passion; they lack safety. Protecting uniqueness means building a safe place for one another to be known, not just impressed.

When couples understand that their covenant is one of a kind, carries an assignment, and deserves protection, comparison loses its voice and stewardship takes over. Stewardship turns marriage from performance into partnership, from pressure into purpose, and from exhaustion into testimony.

Drip-Free Practice: Guarding the Ordinary

For the next seven days, choose one ordinary activity you already do together, such as grocery shopping, cooking, folding laundry, or taking a short walk, and treat it as sacred stewardship rather than routine. Do it without rushing, distraction, or complaint.

Simple acts done with intention seal a covenant better than grand gestures done for display.

Reflection Questions

1. In what ways have you compared your marriage to others (publicly, privately, or silently)?
2. What season do you believe your covenant is currently in (formation, healing, building, stabilizing, or sowing)?
3. What voices, expectations, or pressures have influenced your view of what marriage "should" look like?

4. Where do you see uniqueness in your covenant that you have not previously celebrated?

Application Exercise: Naming Your Assignment

Set aside 30 minutes together this week. Without judgment or interruption, each spouse shares what they believe God has entrusted to your marriage in this season. Consider areas such as family, ministry, finances, creativity, community, work, or healing. After sharing, agree on one small action that aligns with your current assignment and commit to it for the next month.

Prayer

God, thank You for designing our marriage as one of a kind. Help us to release comparison and embrace our unique story, season, and assignment. Teach us to protect our covenant with gentleness, to steward our differences with grace, and to honor the ordinary moments that hold our love together. Guard our unity, align our purpose, and strengthen our testimony. In Jesus' name, Amen.

Affirmation

Our marriage is unique, valuable, and purposeful. We resist comparison, embrace our assignment, and protect what God has entrusted to us.

***

Uniqueness alone does not protect a marriage from erosion. Even the strongest covenants can develop leaks. What often weakens love is not a single collapse, but the quiet accumulation of subtle drips; patterns of neglect, disappointment, and disconnection that go unnoticed until the damage is visible. To safeguard a covenant, those drips must first be recognized.

***

Chapter 2

The Dripping Marriage

***

Introduction to Drips

Every marriage carries moments of tension, disappointment, misunderstanding, and fatigue. These moments are normal because the covenant does not eliminate human complexity. But there is a significant difference between moments and patterns. Moments are brief. Patterns are formative. Moments evaporate. Patterns accumulate. When couples experience negative patterns that accumulate slowly and quietly, those patterns become what we call *drips*. A drip is not a catastrophe. A drip is not betrayal. A drip is not a public scandal. A drip is the slow, subtle erosion of connection over time.

The Subtle Nature of Drips

Drips rarely feel urgent. In fact, most couples do not identify them until much later, when the emotional structure of the relationship has already begun to weaken. When a pipe bursts in a house, everyone notices immediately. Water floods the floors.

Walls crack. Furniture is damaged. Emergency response is required. But when a pipe leaks, no one notices at first. There is no flood. No drama. Nothing demands immediate action. Instead, moisture seeps silently into the wood. It warps support beams. It breeds mold. It compromises structure. Months or years later, what began as an almost invisible drip becomes costly damage. Many marriages do not end because of explosions. They end because of leaks.

What Constitutes a Drip?

A drip in marriage is not a single argument. It is not a bad week. It is not a stressful month. A drip is a repeated experience that goes unacknowledged, unaddressed, and unresolved. Over time, the drip becomes the narrative of the relationship, not by force, but by accumulation.

Common Types of Drips

One of the most common drips is disappointment.

Not disappointment as a singular event, but the quiet accumulation of unmet expectations. When couples first enter marriage, they bring expectations, spoken and unspoken, about affection, communication, finances, roles, spirituality, intimacy, and partnership. Some expectations are rooted in childhood observation.

Others are shaped by culture, ministry, media, or previous relationships. When these expectations are not met, disappointment forms. Most couples do not argue about disappointment immediately. They internalize it. They rationalize it. They tell themselves, maybe things will change later. When later arrives and little has shifted, disappointment becomes resignation. Resignation is simply disappointment that has accepted permanence.

Another drip is silence. Not silence from peace or comfort, but silence from avoidance. Couples often stop communicating honestly, not because they have nothing to say, but because they are tired of how emotions feel when spoken aloud. Avoidance becomes a coping mechanism. Instead of addressing frustrations or needs, couples choose to keep the peace by withholding. Withholding may prevent conflict in the moment, but it prevents connection long-term. You can have peace or connection, but you cannot have both if peace is defined as the absence of discomfort.

There is also the drip of assumption. Assumption occurs when couples believe they know what the other thinks, feels, or intends without asking. Assumption bypasses curiosity.

Curiosity is essential for intimacy because intimacy requires knowing. When knowing is replaced by assumption, the connection shifts from reality to imagination.

The problem is that imagination often interprets through insecurity. Without verification, assumption becomes suspicion, and suspicion becomes narrative. Narrative shapes behavior. Behavior reinforces narrative. A marriage can slowly lose trust without any act of betrayal, simply because imagination replaced conversation.

Neglect is another drip. Neglect is not the absence of love; it is the absence of intentionality. Many couples still love each other deeply but neglect the practices that maintain emotional closeness. They neglect celebration. They neglect affection. They neglect play. They neglect curiosity. They neglect spiritual agreement. They neglect rest. They neglect time. Neglect does not always appear as hostility. Sometimes neglect appears as indifference. *Indifference* is not loud, but it is heavy. Indifference tells the other person, *I am here physically, but I am not here with you.*

Fatigue is a drip that often goes undetected because it feels justified. Modern life exhausts people. Work schedules, financial pressure, commute times, ministry obligations, parental responsibilities, caregiving demands, and cultural expectations create chronic fatigue.

Chronic fatigue makes everything feel urgent except connection. When fatigue becomes the norm, marriage becomes transactional.

Conversations focus on logistics—children, bills, schedules, errands—not intimacy. Logistics are necessary, but logistics cannot substitute for connection.

When logistics become the only conversations couples have, they begin living parallel lives instead of shared ones.

Distraction is a newer drip, made worse by technology. Phones, screens, notifications, social media, and constant information feed create fragmented attention. *Fragmented attention* destroys presence. Presence is the currency of intimacy. Two people can be in the same room and not be together. Two people can share a bed and not share connection. Two people can raise children together and not raise unity. Distraction steals more marriages today than infidelity ever has. Infidelity destroys trust. Distraction erodes the bond.

The Ripple Effect of Drips

Comparison, which we explored in the previous chapter, is a drip that disguises itself as aspiration. Couples believe they are being inspired by others, but often they are being measured by them. Comparison introduces dissatisfaction.

Dissatisfaction introduces resentment. *Resentment* introduces distance. Distance introduces loneliness.

Loneliness introduces temptation. Temptation introduces abandonment of the assignment. Many marriages never collapse because of moral failure; they collapse because of emotional loneliness that remains unspoken.

Resentment itself is a drip. Resentment does not emerge suddenly. It forms slowly, through a pattern of unmet needs, unspoken hurts, or unbalanced burdens. Resentment grows when one spouse feels they are giving more than they are receiving, carrying more than they can sustain, or sacrificing without recognition. Resentment is not poisonous because of volume; it is poisonous because of duration. A small resentment held for a long time can do more damage than a large offense confessed quickly.

Finally, there is the drip of disengagement. *Disengagement* is when a spouse stops trying. Not because they don't care, but because caring feels futile. Attempts to initiate conversation, affection, intimacy, or change are met with indifference or deflection. Over time, the pursuing spouse withdraws. The marriage becomes quiet, efficient, and emotionally uninhabited. On the outside, everything looks peaceful.

On the inside, the marriage is empty. Some marriages end loudly through conflict; others end quietly through disengagement.

The Erosion of Connection

Andre and Keisha experienced several of these drips simultaneously. They were not hostile toward each other. They were not plotting separation. They were not questioning their love. They were experiencing slow erosion.

Andre felt financial pressure and assumed Keisha understood why he was distant, without ever saying so. Keisha felt emotional loneliness and assumed Andre didn't care, without ever asking. They both avoided conversations that felt heavy, hoping things would naturally improve with time. They compared their life to others, not maliciously but honestly.

They were fatigued. They were distracted. They were trying their best. And yet, the drip continued.

The Deceptive Nature of Drips

Drips are dangerous because they are believable. They make couples think erosion is normal. They make resignation feel mature. They make distance feel inevitable. They make loneliness feel justified. They make maintenance feel optional. But Scripture does not present the covenant as something that maintains itself. Covenant requires upkeep.

In Proverbs, we are told: *"Be diligent to know the state of your flocks, and attend to your herds…"* (Proverbs 27:23, NKJV)

This principle applies to relationships. You must know the condition of what has been entrusted to you. You cannot steward what you do not assess, and you cannot repair what you do not acknowledge.

What makes drips even more deceptive is that they rarely produce an immediate crisis. Most couples only seek help during floods; infidelity, separation, emotional collapse, or severe conflict. But by the time a flood occurred, the damage had already been done. The key to a drip-free marriage is not crisis response; it is early detection. Early detection requires awareness. Awareness requires honesty. Honesty requires humility. This humility is not just before God; it is before each other. A marriage cannot heal what both spouses refuse to name.

Most drips are not relational failures; they are formation invitations. Drips reveal where maintenance is needed. Maintenance is not glamorous, but it is holy. Maintenance sustains covenant through seasons. Maintenance is the difference between a house that collapses under a storm and a house that withstands it. Jesus taught: *"A house divided against itself, that house will not be able to stand."* (Mark 3:25, NKJV)

Division does not always appear as conflict. Division often appears as parallel lives under one roof. Protecting the connection is not optional; it is essential. Covenant cannot thrive on autopilot.

The Source of Drips

Drips do not appear without a source. Every pattern has an origin, even if the couple is unaware of it.

Most of the leaks that weaken the covenant begin quietly, long before marriage begins. They begin in family systems, in personal history, in expectations formed by culture, in unhealed wounds, and in unspoken assumptions about love. Marriage does not create these origins; it exposes them. Covenant does not invent pressure; it reveals what pressure has access to.

Common Sources of Drips in Marriage

Every person enters marriage with expectations, what affection should look like, how conflict should be managed, how finances should be stewarded, how intimacy should unfold, how decisions should be made, what roles each person should play, and how spirituality should be expressed. Some expectations are explicit and spoken aloud. Others are implicit, assumed but never articulated. When expectations are unmet, disappointment forms.

When expectations are not communicated, disappointment has no corrective pathway. Disappointment without communication becomes a breeding ground for misunderstanding.

These expectations often originate from the family of origin. Family systems teach us what marriage looks like, either through modeling or through absence. Some grew up witnessing affectionate marriages; others witnessed distance. Some observed shared leadership; others observed hierarchy. Some observed conflict resolution; others observed silent withdrawal. Some witnessed joy; others witnessed survival. Children are astute observers but poor interpreters. They internalize patterns long before they can name them. Those patterns become templates for adult relationships. When a spouse does not match the template, frustration surfaces, not because the spouse is unloving, but because the template was unchallenged.

Another source of the drip is unhealed wounds. Wounds from previous relationships, betrayals, abandonment, rejection, or family trauma do not vanish when vows are spoken. Marriage provides intimacy, and intimacy provides proximity. Proximity gives access to unhealed parts of the soul. This is why marriage can feel both beautiful and threatening; it invites vulnerability. Vulnerability can feel like exposure to someone who has been wounded.

Out of self-protection, wounded spouses may withdraw, avoid emotion, control, or over-function. None of these responses indicates a lack of love; they indicate a lack of healing.

Psychologists use the term *attachment* to describe the way humans form and maintain relationships. Attachment develops in early childhood and influences how adults seek security. While attachment theory can become complex, its basic insight is simple: people love from the place they were formed. Some spouses pursue closeness quickly, often described as *anxious attachment*.

Others protect distance to avoid pain, often described as *avoidant attachment*. Others fluctuate between both. Marriage becomes a laboratory where attachment dynamics play out. Drips often form not because spouses are incompatible, but because their attachment strategies collide without interpretation.

Another origin of the drip is differing conflict strategies. Families teach people how to handle conflict: fight, flee, freeze, fix, or submit. When spouses have opposing strategies, one pursues conversation while the other seeks space. Conflict escalates not from content but from process. The topic may be trivial, but the process is destabilizing. Without awareness, these patterns create a drip of misunderstanding.

One spouse feels unheard; the other feels inundated. One feels abandoned; the other feels attacked. The conflict is not about the topic; it is about the strategy.

Life also applies pressure through finances, children, health challenges, career transitions, ministry demands, and extended family obligations. Stress reduces capacity. Reduced capacity leads to defensive behaviors. Even healthy marriages look strained under chronic stress. Stress does not create the drip, but it increases its speed.

Covenant carries generational, relational, and Kingdom implications. Marriage is not spiritually neutral.

Jesus made it clear that unity is powerful and division is destructive when He taught, *"If a house is divided against itself, that house cannot stand."* (Mark 3:25, NKJV). The enemy rarely attacks marriage directly at first; he attacks unity. Unity can be attacked through discouragement, distraction, division, offense, or resignation. Discouragement tells the couple, *this is too hard.* Distraction tells them that everything else matters more. Division tells them that *you are against each other.* Offense tells them, *you must protect yourself, not your covenant.* Resignation tells them, *this will never change.* None of these assaults requires visible conflict. Most of them operate internally, through thought and perception.

Modern culture glorifies autonomy and self-fulfillment. Marriage, by contrast, requires interdependence and self-sacrifice. When autonomy is idolized, marriage feels restrictive.

When self-fulfillment is idolized, marriage feels disappointing. Culture also glamorizes novelty and stimulation. Marriage, however, thrives on consistency and maintenance. Maintenance is quiet. Novelty is loud. In a culture that honors loudness, maintenance is undervalued.

Technology amplifies cultural pressure. Constant connection to devices reduces connection to spouses. The presence of a phone at the dinner table, the intrusion of notifications during conversation, or the habit of scrolling in bed may seem trivial, but they fracture attention.

Attention is the currency of intimacy. Without attention, intimacy dries up. Without intimacy, a covenant becomes mechanical. Mechanical marriages do not usually break; they rust.

Gender expectations contribute to the drip as well. Many couples adopt roles based on family, culture, or ministry environment that do not fit their assignment or temperament. When roles are mismatched, pressure forms. Pressure leads to resentment. Resentment leads to withdrawal. Withdrawal becomes a drip.

The issue is not whether roles are traditional or modern; the issue is whether roles are aligned with calling, wiring, and season.

Another origin of the drip is a mismatched pace. Couples often begin marriage in sync, only to diverge as life unfolds.

One grows spiritually while the other stagnates. One evolves emotionally while the other remains guarded. One matures financially while the other avoids accountability. One expands socially while the other becomes introverted. Without shared check-ins, pace divergence becomes emotional distance. Not because either spouse is wrong, but because growth happened without agreement.

The Influence of Spiritual Rhythms on Marriage

Spiritual rhythms also influence the drip. Some marriages pray together frequently. Others have silent but deep spiritual lives. Others rely on the church community for spiritual alignment. Others drift from shared spiritual practices entirely. *Spiritual drift* does not always look rebellious.

Often, it looks distracted. The writer of Hebrews warns: *"We must pay much closer attention to what we have heard, lest we drift away from it."* (Hebrews 2:1, ESV) *Drift* is rarely intentional. It is often passive. Drifting marriages do not reject the covenant; they stop tending it.

The Role of Seasons in Marriage

Seasons contribute as well. Marriage has seasons of transition—newlyweds, child-rearing, blended family adjustment, career shifts, caregiving, empty nest, and retirement. Each season introduces both opportunity and strain.

What was effortless in one season becomes difficult in another. Affection, communication, intimacy, and companionship shift with the season. Couples often assume that what was easy should remain easy. When ease disappears, they interpret the change as incompatibility rather than seasonality.

Finally, the expectation of self-sufficiency breeds the drip. Many couples assume they should be able to fix their marriage without help. They believe seeking counsel is weakness or failure. They refuse maintenance until a crisis occurs. Most marriages do not need rescue; they need tuning. *Rescue* happens during floods. *Tuning* happens during drips.

The danger of a drip is not its speed but its trajectory. Drips are slow. Drips are quiet. Drips are believable. Drips seem survivable. But over time, drips reassign meaning inside the marriage.

Meaning is more powerful than moments. People do not respond to what happened; they respond to what they believe happened means. When disappointment accumulates without repair, meaning shifts from *"I wish things were different"* to *"Things will never change."*

When silence accumulates without curiosity, meaning shifts from *"We're tired"* to *"We have nothing to say."*

When assumptions accumulate without verification, meaning shifts from *"I might be wrong"* to *"I already know how you are."*

When neglect accumulates without intentionality, meaning shifts from *"We are busy"* to *"I am alone."*

Consequences of drips

These shifts are subtle at first but devastating over time. Couples rarely collapse because of one argument, one season of stress, or one unresolved tension. Collapse occurs when meaning reshapes identity, when spouses begin to relate to each other not as covenant partners, but as liabilities, strangers, or obstacles.

One of the first effects of a drip over time is *emotional erosion*. *Emotional erosion* is not explosive. It is gradual. It is the quiet diminishing of affection, spontaneity, and tenderness. Small gestures disappear. Curiosity fades. Humor dries up.

Touch becomes rare. Compliments are replaced by critique or silence. Marriage becomes professional instead of personal.

Spouses become coworkers managing a shared enterprise, children, household, finances, or ministry, rather than lovers stewarding intimacy.

Another consequence is *narrative formation*. Every spouse carries an internal narrative about the relationship. Narrative is the lens through which behavior is interpreted. If the narrative becomes pessimistic, neutral actions are interpreted negatively. A spouse coming home late becomes selfishness. A forgotten task becomes disrespect. A request for space becomes a rejection. The situation has not changed; the narrative has.

Narrative shifts are powerful because humans trust their interpretations more than their observations. Once the narrative turns negative, evidence accumulates effortlessly. The drip did not create the negative event; it created the negative lens.

Over time, drips also generate *emotional loneliness*. *Emotional loneliness* is different from physical loneliness. Physical loneliness is the absence of people. *Emotional loneliness* is the absence of connection. Many couples sleep in the same bed, live in the same house, raise the same children, serve in the same ministry, and attend the same church, yet feel profoundly alone in one another's presence.

Emotional loneliness is one of the most painful experiences within a covenant because it violates the very promise of marriage: companionship. Genesis records: *"It is not good for the man to be alone..."* (Genesis 2:18, NKJV)

Aloneness in marriage is not God's design. When *emotional loneliness* settles into a relationship, temptation increases.

Temptation is not always sexual. Sometimes it is emotional—the temptation to confide elsewhere, to escape into work, to anesthetize with entertainment or food, or to build fantasy worlds where needs are met without vulnerability.

Drips also produce *resignation. Resignation* is different from surrender. Surrender stops fighting because peace has been made. *Resignation* stops fighting because hope is lost. *Resignation* transforms requests into silence, complaints into indifference, and desires into apathy. When *resignation* sets in, the marriage becomes functional instead of relational. Functional marriages can survive for decades, but they cannot thrive.

They can raise children, manage homes, serve communities, and participate in churches, but they cannot produce intimacy or joy. They can endure, but they cannot testify.

Another consequence is *disengagement. Disengagement* is the quiet withdrawal of participation. The disengaged spouse stops initiating, stops pursuing, stops asking, stops sharing, and stops risking. They do not necessarily leave physically; they leave emotionally.

Spouses often misinterpret *disengagement* as a lack of love, but *disengagement* is more often a sign of exhaustion than the absence of affection.

People disengage when they conclude that effort will not lead to change. In this way, *disengagement* is a survival strategy, not an act of rebellion.

As drips accumulate, they alter how conflict is experienced. Conflict becomes either constant or non-existent. Constant conflict indicates that connection attempts have not been successful. Non-existent conflict indicates that one or both spouses have stopped trying to connect at all. Conflict is not evidence of a failing marriage; sometimes conflict is evidence that the marriage is still alive. A silent marriage may not be peaceful; it may be depressing.

A persistent drip also affects spiritual life within the marriage. Prayer becomes mechanical or rare. Spiritual conversations diminish. Agreement in decision-making weakens.

Worship becomes individualistic instead of shared. Couples begin to outsource spiritual formation to church services or pastors rather than cultivating shared rhythms at home. The issue is not that the couple is unspiritual; it is that the drip has weakened spiritual unity.

Unity is not automatic. *Unity* is cultivated. Jesus spoke to this when He said: "*If two of you agree here on earth concerning anything you ask, my Father in heaven will do it for you.*" (Matthew 18:19, NLT) *Agreement* is a form of power. Drips weaken agreement.

A house divided does not collapse overnight; it collapses gradually as agreement dissolves.

Over time, drips create vulnerability to external intrusion. Affairs, addictions, excessive work, emotional entanglements, or escapism often begin not with lust or rebellion, but with loneliness and resignation. When emotional oxygen is lacking in marriage, the soul looks for ventilation. This does not justify transgression, but it explains why maintenance matters. Drips create the conditions in which entire covenants can be jeopardized for the promise of temporary relief.

There is also a generational dimension. Children raised in homes with persistent drips learn marriage from observation. They witness narrative, not intention. They absorb resignation, not vows.

They internalize whether marriage is joy or burden, partnership or performance, intimacy or task.

Children formed under the influence of unresolved drips often carry them into their own relationships. In this way, the drip not only erodes the present connection but also influences future family systems. Scripture warns us: *"...for the intention of a man's heart is evil from his youth."* (Genesis 8:21, AMP)

This reminds us that formation begins early and deeply. Marriages are not only covenants, but they are also classrooms.

The Danger of Normalizing Drips

The ultimate danger of the drip is that by the time couples notice the damage, the erosion feels normal. Normalization feels unnecessary. Intervention requires humility, and humility is difficult when a pattern has become familiar.

But familiarity should not be confused with health. Many things can be familiar and harmful: *resentment*, *distance*, overwork, comparison, and silence, among them.

If drips are not addressed, couples reach a threshold where they conclude that the marriage is irreparable. This threshold is less about the severity of the issues and more about the absence of hope.

When hope is lost, the covenant is abandoned. Not always through divorce, sometimes through coexistence.

A marriage can survive legally and die spiritually. In the Kingdom, survival is not the definition of success. *Fruitfulness* is. Jesus taught:

"Every tree that does not bear good fruit is cut down and thrown into the fire." (Matthew 7:19, NIV)

The call of marriage is not mere endurance; it is *fruitfulness*. *Fruitfulness* requires pruning, watering, guarding, and cultivation. None of these activities is dramatic, but all of them are essential.

Repairing the Drip

Drips do not announce themselves with a crisis. They announce themselves with opportunity; the opportunity for repair. Repair is not weakness; *repair is wisdom*.

Repair is how the covenant stays alive. Repair is how fruit is protected. Repair is how testimony is preserved.

Drip-Free Practice: The Two-Question Check-In

Once a week, ask each other two questions:

1. *"What have you needed from me recently?"*
2. *"How can I better show up for you in this season?"*

Listen without defending or explaining. *Curiosity is repair.*

Reflection Questions

1. Which drips have you recognized in your marriage; silence, disappointment, assumption, fatigue, neglect, or disengagement?
2. How have these drips affected your connection, communication, or intimacy?
3. What narratives have formed in your mind about your spouse or your marriage over time?
4. Where have you resigned instead of repaired?

Application Exercise: Mapping the Drip

Individually write down three small areas where you feel erosion has occurred; emotionally, spiritually, or practically. Then share honestly.

Choose one area to address together over the next thirty days. Improvement is not built through grand gestures but through consistent maintenance.

Prayer

Father, thank You for revealing the subtle drips that weaken the covenant. Give us courage to acknowledge what we have ignored, humility to listen without defending, and grace to repair without shame. Heal emotional erosion, restore unity, and revive intimacy where resignation has settled. Make our marriage fruitful, whole, and aligned with Your purposes. In Jesus' name, Amen.

Affirmation

We choose repair over resignation, attention over neglect, and unity over division. Our marriage is worth tending.

***

Drips do not begin in isolation. They are often fed by influences we quietly allow into the marriage; images, comparisons, fantasies, and expectations shaped far beyond the covenant itself. When desire is distorted, connection weakens. Before love can be restored, we must confront what is quietly reshaping it.

CHAPTER 3

A Marriage "Porn Apart"

***

Pornography does not usually enter a marriage with fanfare or crisis. It enters quietly, subtly, and often long before the wedding day. It begins as curiosity, amusement, exploration, stress relief, or distraction, and it follows the individual into adulthood like a hidden companion. Because pornography is typically consumed privately, it forms a relationship with secrecy before it ever intersects with covenant.

Secrecy becomes its first sealant. Shame becomes its second.

Once those two bonds tighten, porn becomes a leak that is both psychological and spiritual, both relational and neurological, both modern and ancient.

Pornography functions as a fantasy drip. It offers arousal without vulnerability, stimulation without relationship, climax without connection, and escape without responsibility. It is sexual activity without emotional investment and intimacy without covenant. The human body responds to porn as a stimulus, while the soul responds to porn as a substitute.

God designed intimacy as a multi-dimensional experience: physical, emotional, relational, and spiritual. Porn collapses all those layers into one: sensation. Sensation is not evil, but sensation alone cannot sustain a covenant. When sensation becomes central and intimacy becomes optional, the marriage begins to drip.

This drip often begins long before the couple recognizes it. For many men, and increasingly for many women, porn becomes a way to manage stress, boredom, insecurity, or loneliness. It becomes an anesthetic.

Anesthetics numb pain but do not heal it.
Anesthetics offer relief but not restoration.

When porn becomes anesthesia, it trains the individual to address internal discomfort without relational engagement. Marriage, on the other hand, requires relational engagement for healing. The two systems are incompatible. One trains the soul to hide; the other requires the soul to be known.

Porn also functions as an escape. Escape is not always rebellion; sometimes it is fatigue. Couples overwhelmed by work, family demands, ministry responsibilities, financial pressure, or emotional tension may seek escape from their own lives.

Porn offers a low-cost, high-stimulation exit from stress without negotiation. No one has to talk. No one has to compromise.

No one has to wait. No one has to show up as their imperfect self. The body receives dopamine without delay; the mind receives distraction without vulnerability.

But escape has consequences. When escape becomes habitual, presence becomes optional. And a covenant cannot thrive without presence.

Part of the power of pornography lies in novelty. The human brain releases dopamine not primarily in response to pleasure, but in anticipation of novelty and reward. Porn provides endless novelty: new faces, new bodies, new scenarios, new fantasies, on demand.

This creates a neurological drip.

The brain becomes accustomed to high-stimulation novelty loops, while real-life intimacy requires familiarity, patience, and repetition. Novelty trains the brain; covenant trains the heart. When novelty dominates the nervous system, familiarity feels boring. Boredom breeds dissatisfaction. Dissatisfaction fuels secrecy. Secrecy sustains the drip.

Secrecy is not merely hiding; secrecy is the absence of a witness. God designed the covenant to be witnessed by spouses, by the community, and by heaven.

Porn dismantles witness by disconnecting sexuality from relationship.

No one knows.

No one sees.

No one shares.

No one interprets.

The activity is contained, but the consequences are not. Secrecy forms a drip because secrecy fractures unity. Unity is not only physical alignment; it is shared life. Secrecy removes a part of life from the partnership and stores it in the shadows.

The enemy works in shadows because shadows prevent confession, and confession leads to restoration.

Shame reinforces secrecy. Shame whispers,

If they knew, they would reject you.
If they knew, you would disappoint them.
If they knew, you would be disqualified.

Shame lies. Shame isolates. Shame convinces the believer that their weakness is incompatible with grace.

Yet Scripture declares:

"There is now no condemnation for those who are in Christ Jesus..." (Romans 8:1, NIV)

Condemnation and shame are not the same. Condemnation attacks identity. Shame attacks belonging.

When shame lodges itself within a marriage, it stops vulnerability. Vulnerability is one of the currencies of intimacy.

When vulnerability shuts down, intimacy dries up. Intimacy drying up is a drip.

Pornography also creates unrealistic expectations. The sexual scripts presented in pornography are exaggerated, choreographed, edited, and detached from emotional context. When these scripts become internalized as normal, real intimacy feels insufficient. Distance is a drip.

Availability, Shame, and the Internal Rewiring

Women are often shocked to learn that porn is frequently not about beauty. It is about availability. Porn is not more beautiful than a spouse; it is more accessible. Accessibility without vulnerability is addictively efficient.

In marriage, accessibility requires pursuit, intentionality, and emotional investment. Porn removes all those ingredients.

Porn gives the reward without the road. But rewards without roads produce counterfeit intimacy.

The drip becomes even more pronounced when pornography intersects with spiritual formation.

Many believers assume porn consumption is purely a moral failure. While it is sinful and destructive, reducing it to morality alone misses its complexity.

Porn is neurological, psychological, cultural, and relational.

If we treat porn only as a moral problem, we will apply only moral solutions: shame, silence, suppression. None of these produces healing. Healing requires understanding. Understanding produces compassion. Compassion produces courage. Courage produces confession. Confession produces connection. Connection produces restoration.

Scripture reminds us:

"Confess your sins to each other and pray for each other so that you may be healed." (James 5:16, NLT)

Confession is not merely a ritual; it is a repair mechanism.

Andre struggled with pornography in silence for years. He assumed Keisha would be devastated if she knew. He assumed his struggle disqualified him from spiritual leadership and from sexual connection. He tried to quit repeatedly through willpower, but willpower without support eventually buckled.

Meanwhile, Keisha interpreted Andre's distance as disinterest. She did not see shame; she saw rejection. She did not see secrecy; she saw avoidance. She did not see fatigue; she saw withdrawal.

Neither of them was correct, but both were affected.

The drip was not just sexual; it was emotional, spiritual, and relational.

The longer porn remains unaddressed, the more it rewires the internal reward system. Rewiring affects attention, arousal patterns, preference, and emotional bonding. Porn does not simply stimulate the body; it trains the brain.

Marriage requires bonding.

Bonding requires presence.

Presence requires vulnerability.

Porn replaces presence with fantasy and vulnerability with control. This drip reshapes the covenant from within.

Secrecy produces shame, and shame produces silence. Shame is not merely guilt; shame is identity distortion.

Guilt says, *I did something wrong.*

Shame says, *Something is wrong with me.*

Shame convinces spouses they are unworthy of understanding, forgiveness, or intimacy. Shame is also deeply spiritual.

Scripture describes shame entering the world immediately after sin:

"Then the eyes of both were opened... and they sewed fig leaves together and made themselves coverings." (Genesis 3:7, NKJV)

Covering is the instinctive response to shame. Porn creates coverings within marriage, digital fig leaves. But coverings prevent connection. Marriage requires nakedness, not merely physical, but emotional and spiritual. Porn encourages hiding.

Division, Disengagement, and the Spiritual Fracture

The neurological consequences also shape covenant. Porn stimulates dopamine surges that reinforce novelty-seeking behavior. Marriage, however, is built on familiarity. Familiarity is not a flaw; it is a feature. Deep love emerges through repeated experiences, shared history, and consistent presence.

When novelty is prioritized neurologically, familiarity feels like a deficiency. This can create a drip of boredom within the covenant that has nothing to do with the spouse and everything to do with dopamine tolerance.

Pornography also affects sexual rhythm. Some spouses become less interested in sex with their partner, not because they lack attraction, but because their sexual energy has already been expended privately. In other cases, porn increases sexual expectation in ways that feel overwhelming to the partner. Both patterns disrupt the mutual nature of intimacy. Mutuality is a covenant concept. One-sided sexuality fragments unity.

Another relational consequence is emotional displacement. Porn is often used to manage emotions: loneliness, stress, fear, insecurity, anxiety, or even spiritual discouragement. When porn becomes a coping mechanism, the marriage loses the opportunity to become a safe place for emotional processing. Spouses stop turning toward each other and start turning inward. Turning inward is a form of relational abandonment, even if unintentional.

Spiritual consequences must also be acknowledged. Pornography introduces division.

Division does not always happen through arguments; sometimes it happens through secrecy, shame, and isolation. Jesus warned:

"Every... house divided against itself will not stand." (Matthew 12:25, NKJV)

Division weakens covenant authority. Authority in marriage is expressed through agreement. When porn introduces betrayal, even unspoken betrayal, agreement fractures. Fractured agreement weakens prayer, weakens discernment, weakens unity, and weakens spiritual covering.

There is also an enemy strategy at play. The enemy rarely initiates destruction through dramatic events. He begins through isolation. Isolation makes the soul susceptible to accusation. Accusation produces condemnation. Condemnation produces resignation. Resignation abandons the pursuit. Once pursuit dies, intimacy follows.

Intimacy is not just sex; intimacy is knowing and being known. Porn replaces knowing with viewing and replaces being known with hiding.

Porn also impacts sexual confidence. When spouses discover pornography, they often internalize the event as personal rejection.

The betrayed spouse may ask:

Why wasn't I enough?

What do they see in that that they don't see in me?

Are they dissatisfied with me?

These questions strike at the core of sexual identity. Sexual identity within marriage is tender. Porn attacks tenderness by introducing comparison and insecurity without explanation.

For the spouse consuming porn, confidence also collapses. They may feel unworthy of intimacy, unqualified for spiritual leadership, or disqualified from affection. Sexual shame often becomes spiritual shame. They stop praying. They stop confessing. They stop pursuing. They stop initiating. They stop hoping. Porn becomes not just sexual sin, but spiritual resignation.

Over time, the most profound effect of porn on marriage is not sexual at all; it is relational disengagement. The individual no longer needs their spouse for sexual connection. The marriage loses not only participation, but also partnership. Porn makes covenant optional in the bedroom. Optionality is poison to the covenant. Covenant thrives on exclusivity. Porn introduces a third presence into a space meant for two.

Andre and Keisha reached this point quietly. Andre stopped initiating affection because shame made him feel unworthy. Keisha stopped initiating intimacy because she interpreted Andre's distance as rejection. Neither was correct, but both were wounded. The drip had become a leak, not through scandal, but through secrecy.

Repair, Agreement, and Drip-Free Practice

Repairing the porn leak in covenant requires more than shame, secrecy, or suppression. Suppression is not repentance, and shame is not transformation. Pornography thrives in darkness; healing thrives in witness. Witness does not mean public exposure; it means relational participation. In marriage, that participation begins with honesty, courage, and grace.

The first movement of repair is confession. Confession is not just an admission of behavior; it is the reintroduction of witness. Confession disrupts secrecy, breaks isolation, and creates an on-ramp for grace. Confession is not about humiliation, but about restoration. Scripture declares:

"Confess your sins to each other and pray for each other so that you may be healed."- (James 5:16, NLT)

Notice: confession does not merely bring forgiveness; it brings healing.

Many spouses have been forgiven privately by God but remain unhealed because secrecy prevents relational and spiritual witness.

Confession without repentance is manipulation. Confession with repentance leads to transformation.

After confession comes compassion. Compassion does not mean excusing sin; it means understanding the struggle without resorting to humiliation or moral superiority. Porn is rarely defeated through condemnation. Condemnation fuels shame. Shame fuels secrecy. Secrecy fuels relapse. Porn requires both accountability and empathy. Accountability without empathy crushes. Empathy without accountability enables. Covenant requires both.

The next movement of repair is agreement. An agreement means both spouses decide that this leak will be confronted as a team, not as adversaries. The enemy wants spouses on opposite sides of the struggle, one as the guilty party, the other as the judge. Covenant puts both on the same side against the leak. Agreement transforms porn from a marital wedge into a marital mission.

Practically, repair involves guardrails. Guardrails are not signs of weakness; they are signs of stewardship. In every other area of life, we recognize the necessity of guardrails: financial budgets, dietary plans, time boundaries, and digital filters..

Sexual guardrails protect what is sacred. Guardrails may include accountability software, device limits, content restrictions, or changes in digital habits. These are not punishments; they are protections.

Repair also includes rewiring intimacy. Porn trains the body and brain to expect arousal without relationship. Marriage requires arousal through a relationship. Rewiring intimacy means rebuilding connection through conversation, affection, vulnerability, spiritual agreement, and non-sexual touch. Many couples attempt to repair porn damage through sexual frequency alone, but frequency cannot repair what disconnection has damaged. Intimacy is not measured in acts, but in atmosphere.

Scripture admonishes:

"Be kind to each other, tenderhearted, forgiving one another, just as God through Christ has forgiven you." (Ephesians 4:32, NLT)

Forgiveness must be accompanied by rebuilding. Rebuilding takes time. Time requires patience. Patience requires hope. Hope requires testimony. Testimony is what happens when a marriage refuses to let the leak define the covenant.

Porn does not need to be the end of the covenant. It can become the beginning of deeper unity.

The drip can be sealed.

The leak can be repaired.

Covenants can be restored.

Grace is not merely pardon; grace is empowerment.

Porn may have introduced secrecy, but covenant introduces agreement. Agreement is stronger than fantasy. Agreement is stronger than shame. Agreement is stronger than isolation. The question is not whether the leak existed; the question is whether the leak will be addressed.

Drip-Free Practice

Replace Hidden with Witness. This week, choose one area where secrecy has lived and intentionally replace it with witness. This may involve sharing struggles, digital habits, or emotional burdens. Witness breaks isolation.

Reflection Questions

1. How has pornography or fantasy displaced intimacy, attention, or connection within your marriage?
2. What would repair require: confession, compassion, agreement, guardrails, or pursuit?

Application Exercise

Craft a Covenant Guardrail

Together, identify one boundary that protects intimacy, digital, emotional, or relational, and agree to practice it for 30 days. Guardrails preserve covenant; they do not restrict it.

Prayer

Father, thank You for being present in the places we hide. Give us courage to confess, compassion to listen, and grace to repair. Break shame, lift condemnation, and restore intimacy. Seal the leaks that secrecy created and strengthen the unity that the covenant requires. In Jesus' name, Amen.

Affirmation

We choose honesty over hiding, agreement over isolation, and pursuit over resignation. Our covenant is worth protecting.

***

Not all leaks are born of fantasy. Some grow quietly through distraction, through work, ambition, ministry, and even good intentions that slowly crowd out connection. When couples begin living parallel rather than together, retreat can feel safer than repair. What begins as busyness can end in distance.

***

Chapter 4
Rooftop Living: When Couples Retreat Instead of Connect

***

Some marriages end with explosions, arguments, or obvious fractures. Others end with distance. Distance rarely announces itself with crisis. It enters quietly, like fatigue or distraction, and takes up residence in the spaces where conversation and affection once lived. Distance is not necessarily hostility. In many marriages, distance appears polite, civil, and functional. It respects boundaries, shares responsibilities, and maintains routines. It may even appear successful to those looking from the outside. But beneath the surface, connection has been replaced by coexistence, and intimacy by parallel living.

The Metaphor of the Roof: A Biblical Perspective

Scripture gives us a metaphor for this pattern in the story of David and Bathsheba. Before the scandal ever occurred, a detail is offered that many overlook:

"In the spring, at the time when kings go off to war... David remained in Jerusalem." (2 Samuel 11:1, NIV)

David was not where the covenant demanded him to be. His body remained in Jerusalem; his assignment remained on the battlefield. David retreated to the roof. The roof became the place where responsibility was abandoned, vulnerability was avoided, and temptation found invitation. The rooftop is where withdrawal becomes opportunity for erosion. For David, the erosion showed up through adultery. For marriages today, the erosion shows up through distance.

Rooftop Living: Retreating from Connection

Rooftop living in marriage is the quiet decision to retreat from intimacy and connection rather than engage discomfort or vulnerability. It is not necessarily malicious; often it is protective. Spouses climb onto the rooftop when the emotional interior of the marriage feels too overwhelming, too critical, too demanding, or too exhausting. The rooftop becomes a refuge from conflict, a sanctuary from disappointment, or a shield against vulnerability. But what feels like refuge eventually becomes exile.

Consider Mark and Alana. They married young, built careers, raised two children, and served faithfully in their church.

They did not fight often. They did not insult each other. They did not sabotage the marriage. They simply stopped pursuing each other. Mark spent more time in his home office, scrolling through financial news and responding to work messages late into the night.

Alana spent more time with the children, coordinating schedules, homework, and church responsibilities. When they were together, their conversations revolved around logistics, school forms, meal plans, ministry events, and bills. Everything was functional. Nothing was intimate.

The Forms of Rooftop Living

Rooftop living manifests in several forms.

- **Retreat into Work**: Work is predictable, structured, and rewarding. It offers metrics, achievement, and affirmation. Fulfillment becomes easier to access there than through the complexities of intimacy.

- **Retreat into Ministry**: Ministry offers spiritual significance and community affirmation. It also offers an excuse for emotional absence that sounds righteous: "I'm serving the Lord." Yet the Lord never asked us to serve others at the expense of our spouse.

- **Retreat into Parenting**: Children require immediate attention and tangible effort. Parenting can absorb emotional energy and create a sense of purpose that distracts from marital emptiness.

- **Retreat into Technology**: The device becomes a rooftop. It provides escape from conversation and immersion without engagement.

- **Retreat Inward or Outward**: Some spouses retreat inward, becoming quiet, withdrawn, and emotionally flat. Others retreat outward, filling their schedules with activities, obligations, and social commitments.

Rooftop Living as a Seasonal Coping Strategy

Rooftop living is often seasonal. It emerges during periods of stress, grief, or transition. After a miscarriage, during a job loss, after a parental death, during burnout, after ministry wounds. The rooftop becomes a temporary coping strategy. But temporary coping strategies, when left unexamined, become permanent living arrangements.

The tragedy of rooftop living is that many couples normalize it. They say, "This is just how marriage becomes after kids," or "This is what happens in long-term relationships," or "We are just in a busy season." But seasons with no intentional return plan become lifestyles. Lifestyles become identity. Identity shapes destiny.

The Erosion of Intimacy: How Distance Feeds the Drip

Rooftop living erodes covenant slowly. It siphons off curiosity. Curiosity is essential for intimacy. Without curiosity, spouses stop asking questions that matter:

- *What are you feeling?*
- *What are you afraid of?*
- *What are you dreaming about now?*
- *What are you carrying in this season?*
- *How can I show up for you?*

When curiosity vanishes, intimacy suffocates. Intimacy rarely dies from hostility; it dies from neglect. Mark and Alana did not notice the rooftop at first. They noticed only fatigue. Fatigue turned into silence. Silence turned into avoidance. Avoidance turned into logistical partnership. Partnership turned into loneliness. Loneliness turned into resignation.

They never fought for divorce; they simply stopped fighting for intimacy. Their marriage became a beautifully decorated rooftop, pleasant, presentable, and elevated, yet disconnected from covenant's interior.

The Reasons Behind Retreat

Spouses rarely retreat without reason. Withdrawal may look passive on the surface, but beneath it are complex dynamics that shape how a person copes, protects, or survives relational tension.

The rooftop is not built in a day. It is constructed over time, through disappointments, misunderstandings, unspoken hurts, unresolved conflicts, and competing responsibilities. Each spouse builds their rooftop for reasons that feel legitimate in the moment, even if those reasons become corrosive over time.

Fatigue: The Silent Retreat

One reason spouses retreat is fatigue. Fatigue accumulates through work, parenting, ministry, caregiving, financial strain, or emotional labor. Fatigue is not always present as anger or sadness; sometimes it shows up as numbness. Numbness is the absence of emotional energy. When numbness takes over, connection feels costly, and withdrawal feels efficient.

Spouses retreat not because they no longer care, but because they no longer have the capacity.

Marriage requires capacity, and capacity requires rest. Without rest, rooftop living becomes a coping mechanism.

Fear of Conflict: Protection Through Withdrawal

Another reason spouses retreat is the fear of conflict. Some individuals grew up in homes where conflict was destructive, loud, punitive, or unpredictable. Others grew up in homes where conflict was nonexistent, silent, suppressed, or avoided. Both environments teach that direct engagement is dangerous. When conflict is feared, rooftop living becomes a protective strategy. It is safer to climb upward and disengage than to descend inward and risk being hurt or misunderstood. Some spouses retreat because they prefer peace over intimacy. Intimacy requires negotiation, honesty, and vulnerability. Peace, defined as the absence of tension, can be achieved through avoidance. Many couples unconsciously trade intimacy for peace. The problem is that peace without intimacy eventually becomes distance, and distance hollows out covenant.

Scripture warns us:

"If possible, so far as it depends on you, live at peace with everyone." (Romans 12:18, ESV)

Peace is good, but peace is not intimacy. Peace is external; intimacy is internal. Peace without intimacy is coexistence.

Shame: The Retreat Caused by Inadequacy

Some spouses retreat because of shame. Shame is not always connected to sin; sometimes it is connected to inadequacy. A spouse may feel inadequate emotionally, financially, spiritually, or sexually. Shame whispers, "*You are failing. You are not enough.* You are disappointing them."

Rather than risk exposure, the spouse withdraws. Shame pushes them to the rooftop, where hiding feels safer than vulnerability. Yet in the Kingdom, shame is never a tool of the Holy Spirit. Conviction draws us toward connection; shame drives us toward isolation.

Retreat can also be rooted in the the avoidance of disappointment. When repeated attempts at connection are ignored, minimized, or misunderstood, spouses may conclude that pursuit is pointless. They stop initiating conversation, affection, or intimacy, not because they have stopped loving, but because they have stopped hoping. Hopelessness is a quiet rooftop builder. It does not shout. It does not accuse. It simply resigns.

Emotional Labor Imbalance: The Source of Retreat

Another reason spouses retreat is unbalanced emotional labor. Every relationship requires emotional labor, processing feelings, maintaining connection, resolving tension, and initiating vulnerability. When one spouse carries most of this labor, they eventually burn out. Burnout produces rooftop living. The burned-out spouse withdraws because they have spent their emotional energy trying to sustain the marriage alone. Meanwhile, the other spouse may interpret the withdrawal as rejection rather than exhaustion. Misinterpretation becomes part of the drip.

Family of Origin Influence: Shaping Retreat Patterns

Family of origin modeling also shapes retreat patterns. Individuals raised in homes where emotional expression was discouraged learn to self-regulate privately. Those raised in homes where vulnerability was mocked learn to protect themselves through withdrawal. Those raised in highly independent environments may view reliance on a spouse as a weakness. Family systems do not determine destiny, but they shape instinct. Instinct influences rooftop patterns.

Attachment styles contribute as well. The anxiously attached spouse fears abandonment and pursues connection aggressively. The avoidantly attached spouse fears engulfment and seeks distance.

When these two marry, rooftop living becomes almost inevitable unless awareness and repair strategies are learned. The avoidant spouse retreats to the rooftop to prevent emotional overload. The anxious spouse chases the rooftop in pursuit of reassurance. Both are trying to protect themselves; neither feels understood.

Personality Differences: Strategies for Coping

Personality differences also play a role. Introverted spouses may retreat to the rooftop to recover from overstimulation. Extroverted spouses may retreat to social environments outside the marriage to alleviate loneliness. Analytical spouses may retreat into problem-solving. Creative spouses may retreat into imagination. None of these are sins; they are strategies. But when strategies replace intimacy, rooftop living emerges.

Spiritual Discouragement: A Spiritual Retreat

Some retreats are spiritual. Discouragement can cause spouses to disengage from the marriage, not because they disbelieve in the covenant, but because they disbelieve in change.

Discouragement convinces the heart that effort is pointless. When discouragement pairs with self-sufficiency, a hallmark of modern culture, spouses begin to solve problems alone rather than together.

The marital table is abandoned not through rebellion but through resignation.

Ministry and Retreat: The Danger of Prioritizing Purpose

There are also ministry-related retreats. Ministry can become a rooftop when spouses prioritize spiritual assignments over marital responsibility.

The rooftop becomes a place where purpose is pursued while covenant is neglected. Ministry should never become the rooftop from which the covenant is abandoned. Ministry flows best from marriage, not over it. Scripture reminds us:

"And the two shall become one flesh."" (Genesis 2:24, KJV)

Ministry is corporate, but covenant is intimate. When the public assignment receives more attention than the private covenant, rooftop living becomes normalized.

Cultural Narratives and Retreat: Glorifying Autonomy

Cultural narratives shape retreat as well. Modern society glorifies autonomy, independence, and self-actualization. Marriage, however, requires interdependence, sacrifice, and mutual submission.

Autonomous individuals can excel in careers, leadership, and ministry while failing in intimacy. Culture trains people to climb ladders, platforms, and titles, but rarely trains them to stay at the table of the covenant.

The table is where emotions are processed, dreams are shared, burdens are transferred, and desires are articulated. The rooftop is where individuals remain in control of their own narrative without interruption.

Finally, spouses retreat to the rooftop because the interior of the marriage feels dangerous. It is not physically dangerous, but emotionally. Emotional danger emerges when vulnerability has been punished, minimization has been normalized, or empathy has been absent. Without empathy, spouses stop sharing their inner worlds. Without sharing, intimacy suffocates. Without intimacy, a covenant becomes a duty. Duty without delight is sustainable for a season, but not for a lifetime.

Mark and Alana's Example: Drifting to the Rooftop

Mark and Alana did not choose the rooftop deliberately. They drifted there through fatigue, avoidance, insecurity, and cultural reinforcement. They assumed their distance was normal.

They assumed stability was the goal. They assumed children and ministry were sufficient evidence of covenant health.

They did not recognize that retreating from each other was slowly transforming their marriage from companionship into coexistence.

Rooftop Living: A Temporary Retreat That Becomes Permanent

Rooftop living is not irreversible. Withdrawal may feel entrenched, but covenant was designed with built-in mechanisms for repair. In Scripture, the rooftop was never meant to be a permanent dwelling place. It was a place for hiding, watching, praying, or grieving—but not for living.

Covenant life happens at tables, not rooftops. Tables represent presence, communion, nourishment, and agreement. Covenant is sustained through presence, and presence requires descent.

The Repair Process: Steps to Descend from the Rooftop

Step 1: Awareness

The first step off the rooftop is awareness. Many couples do not realize they are living on rooftops because rooftop living feels safer than the interior of the marriage. Safety is addictive. But safety without intimacy becomes loneliness.

Awareness means naming where you have retreated and why. It means admitting, "I have withdrawn," or "I have stopped pursuing," or "I have been afraid." Naming the rooftop breaks denial. Denial fuels distance; awareness fuels repair.

Step 2: Invitation

Repair does not begin with demand; it begins with invitation. Demand produces defensiveness. Invitation produces openness. Invitation is the language of pursuit:

- "Can we talk about how we've been distant?"
- "Can we set aside time to reconnect?"
- "I miss us."

Pursuit is not a sign of weakness; it is a sign of covenant. God pursues His bride. Christ pursues the Church. Pursuit is the pattern of love.

Step 3: Curiosity

Curiosity is the antidote to assumption. Assumption kills intimacy; curiosity revives it. Curiosity asks:

- "What has this season felt like for you?"

- "Where have you felt alone?"
- "What are you carrying that I have not seen?"

Curiosity is a form of honor. It communicates, "Your interior world matters to me." Without curiosity, spouses remain strangers beneath the same roof.

Step 4: Safety

Safety is not the absence of conflict; it is the presence of compassion. Safety allows honesty to exist without punishment. Many spouses descend from the rooftop only to retreat again because honesty was met with criticism or dismissal. Safety requires listening to understand, not listening to correct. It requires validation, not minimization. Jesus modeled this when He sat at tables with sinners, doubters, and outcasts. He did not correct first; He connected first.

Step 5: Restoring Shared Rhythms

A critical part of leaving the rooftop is restoring shared rhythms. Rooftop living thrives in separation—separate schedules, separate routines, separate digital lives, separate burdens. Tables are built through shared rhythms:

- Shared meals.
- Shared prayer.
- Shared rest.
- Shared goals.
- Shared play.
- Shared dreams.
- Shared Sabbath.

When rhythms are shared, unity has scaffolding. When rhythms are separate, unity erodes.

Step 6: Mutual Pursuit

One spouse cannot pull the other off the rooftop alone. Pursuit must eventually become reciprocal. In many marriages, one spouse becomes the emotional leader, initiating conversation, repair, and affection. This is honorable, but if it remains unilateral, exhaustion sets in. The roof comes down when mutual pursuit returns. Pursuit does not always look dramatic. Sometimes it looks like attention. Attention is the currency of intimacy.

Step 7: Forgiveness

Forgiveness is often part of descending. Withdrawal wounds. Not because it is loud, but because it feels like abandonment. Abandonment is the deepest relational wound. Forgiveness does not dismiss the wound; it removes the barrier to re-entry. Without forgiveness, the rooftop becomes fortified. With forgiveness, the ladder appears.

Step 8: Repentance

Finally, repentance may be required. Repentance is not merely apology; it is directional change. It is choosing to reenter covenant intentionally rather than remain in safe isolation. Repentance is not just vertical toward God; it is horizontal toward spouse.

Repentance communicates, "I will show up where I previously withdrew. I will descend from safety into connection."

Mark and Alana's Journey of Repair

Mark and Alana began descending gradually. Mark initiated a weekly lunch date away from work distractions. Alana shared that she felt lonely during evenings when Mark immersed himself in his laptop. Mark listened without defense. They began praying briefly together before bed, sometimes for one minute.

Prayer became a table. Conversation returned slowly. Laughter returned later. Intimacy returned eventually. They did not rebuild everything overnight. Descent is rarely instantaneous, but it is always possible.

God rarely meets couples on the rooftop. The rooftop is where we hide. The table is where He communes.

David fled to rooftops in fear, but God prepared tables in the presence of enemies (Psalm 23:5). Jesus ate at tables with sinners, disciples, and skeptics. Revelation ends with a marriage supper, not a rooftop vigil. Covenant is sustained at tables.

Descent from the rooftop is not merely relational, it is spiritual. It transforms marriage from coexistence to communion. Communion requires presence. Presence is costly, but the cost produces reward. Covenant was not designed for survival; it was designed for fruitfulness. Fruitfulness requires descent.

This week, create one shared rhythm—one meal, one walk, one coffee, one prayer, one evening without screens. Tables do not need grandeur; they need consistency.

Reflection Questions

1. In what ways have you or your spouse retreated to a rooftop in this season?
2. What would descent require—awareness, invitation, curiosity, safety, rhythms, or repentance?

Application Exercise: Build a Rhythm

Agree on one recurring rhythm that rebuilds presence (weekly meal, nightly check-in, shared prayer, etc.) and practice it for four weeks. Rhythms build intimacy.

Prayer

Father, give us the courage to descend from the rooftops we have built. Heal the fatigue, fear, disappointment, and shame that led us there. Restore curiosity, presence, and pursuit within our covenant. Bring us back to the table of intimacy and unity. In Jesus' name, Amen.

Affirmation

We choose presence over withdrawal, pursuit over avoidance, and covenant over isolation.

***

Retreating is Not Always Deliberate. Sometimes couples withdraw not because they no longer care, but because they no longer understand one another. Distance grows quietly when efforts are misread and longings go unnamed. Before connection can be restored, love must be translated.

***

Chapter 5

What a Man Wants / What a Woman Wants

***

They were both trying, and that was the tragedy.

He stopped at the grocery store on his way home, remembering the specific brand of snack she liked. He made sure the tank was full, the bills were paid, and the children's homework was checked. He believed, sincerely, that these acts spoke clearly: *I care about you. I am thinking about you. I am carrying this with you.* When he walked through the door that evening, tired but proud of his effort, he expected a sense of shared warmth.

She saw what he had done. She thanked him. But later, as the dishes were put away and the house settled into silence, something still felt unsettled inside her. She did not feel chosen. She did not feel emotionally held.

What she longed for was not logistical competence but emotional presence, a conversation that lingered, a look that said, *You matter beyond what you do.* The groceries were thoughtful. The assistance was helpful. Yet her heart remained slightly untouched.

On another weekend, he spent hours repairing what was broken around the house. He tightened hinges, fixed a cabinet door, and replaced a light fixture that had been flickering for months. To him, this was love expressed in responsibility. He was protecting the home. He was maintaining what they had built together. He was proving reliability.

Meanwhile, she had been hoping that at some point he would sit down beside her without distraction, ask about the thoughts she had been carrying all week, and listen without rushing to solve them. When he finally sat down, exhausted, she felt both grateful and disappointed. Neither was wrong. Neither was selfish. They were loving in the language they understood. And that is where many marriages quietly begin to leak.

The early stages of romance often disguise this problem because desire covers misinterpretation. In courtship, both partners tend to stretch beyond their natural rhythms. He talks more than usual. She adapts more than usual. Effort is high, curiosity is active, and small misunderstandings are forgiven quickly because the emotional climate is warm.

But marriage introduces familiarity, and familiarity reveals default patterns. Over time, people revert to the emotional dialect that feels most natural to them.

The issue is not that men and women are incapable of understanding each other. The issue is that they often assume their own emotional dialect is universal.

Emotional Dialects: Why We Don't Speak the Same Language

When a wife says, "We never talk anymore," she is rarely referring to the exchange of information. She is describing the absence of felt connection. She may want to explore feelings, experiences, spiritual questions, or relational dynamics—not to criticize, but to feel close. When a husband hears this complaint, however, he may instinctively interpret it as failure. He may believe she is implying that he is inadequate, inattentive, or incompetent. In response, he may defend himself or withdraw, reinforcing her original sense of distance.

Similarly, when a husband reaches for physical intimacy after a long week, he may be expressing more than desire. For many men, sexual closeness is intertwined with reassurance, affirmation, and relational safety. It is not only about physical release; it is about connection embodied.

If his advance is declined repeatedly without conversation, he may not merely feel sexually frustrated. He may feel unwanted. She, on the other hand, may be declining not because she rejects him, but because she feels emotionally unseen and therefore unable to relax into vulnerability. Each spouse interprets the other's behavior through their own internal framework, and both can walk away feeling misunderstood. This is what happens when love is offered but not translated.

Scripture does not pretend that this challenge does not exist. When Peter instructs husbands to "live with your wives in an understanding way" (1 Peter 3:7, ESV), he implies that understanding requires effort. It is something cultivated. It is something learned. It is not automatic. Likewise, Proverbs declares, "Through wisdom a house is built, and by understanding it is established" (Proverbs 24:3, NKJV). Understanding stabilizes what love alone begins.

Many couples assume that because they love each other, they should instinctively understand each other. When that instinct fails, they conclude something is wrong with the marriage. In reality, what is often missing is not love but interpretation.

Misinterpretation of Actions: A Male and Female Reflex

Men and women frequently approach conflict differently as well. A wife who senses emotional disconnection may pursue conversation with urgency. Her tone may intensify not because she desires combat, but because she fears distance. A husband who senses rising emotion may retreat, not because he does not care, but because he feels overwhelmed or unprepared. This pursue-withdraw pattern has been documented in relational research for decades. Without awareness, it becomes a predictable cycle: the more she pursues, the more he withdraws; the more he withdraws, the more she escalates. Both believe they are responding reasonably. Both feel increasingly alone.

The Root Fears in Marriage: Emotional Abandonment vs. Inadequacy

What sits beneath these patterns are often unspoken fears.

For many women, the deepest fear in marriage is emotional abandonment, the fear of being unseen, unheard, or left alone emotionally, even while physically together. For many men, the deepest fear is inadequacy, the fear of failing, disappointing, or being exposed as not enough.

When her fear of abandonment collides with his fear of inadequacy, small conflicts take on disproportionate weight. A simple disagreement about scheduling can trigger a much older anxiety about worth or belonging.

Hiding vs. Reaching

In Genesis, after shame entered the world, Adam hid. Hiding is still a common male reflex when shame is activated. Eve, by contrast, reached and spoke. Reaching is still a common female reflex when connection feels threatened. These are not rigid categories, but they are recognizable tendencies. Without understanding, hiding feels like indifference, and reaching feels like an attack.

When Love Misses the Mark

When love consistently misses its mark, discouragement settles in quietly. Each spouse begins to narrate the other in less generous ways. "He doesn't care." "She's never satisfied." These internal narratives harden over time, and hardened narratives are difficult to reverse. What began as a misinterpretation slowly becomes an assumption. When love consistently misses its mark, discouragement settles in quietly.

Each spouse begins to narrate the other in less generous ways. *"He doesn't care." "She's never satisfied."* These internal narratives harden over time, and hardened narratives are difficult to reverse. What began as misinterpretation slowly becomes assumption.

The good news is that assumptions can be examined.

Marriage: A Lifelong Practice of Learning

Marriage is not a compatibility test that you either pass or fail. It is a lifelong practice of learning how the person you love experiences love. It is the humility to admit, *"The way I give may not be the way you receive."* It is the courage to ask, *"What does this mean to you?"* before reacting. When couples learn to interpret rather than assume, frustration decreases. When they slow down enough to ask what longing lies beneath a complaint, empathy begins to replace defensiveness. And when empathy grows, leaks are sealed before resentment can spread.

Understanding does not eliminate difference. It dignifies it.

What a Man Wants: Respect

What a man wants and what a woman wants are not mysteries hidden in abstraction. They are patterns rooted in how each experiences love, respect, safety, and connection.

When most men speak about marriage, they do not begin with vulnerability. They begin with responsibility. They talk about work, providing, fixing, building, and protecting. It is not that they lack emotion; it is that their emotional world is often expressed through competence. For many husbands, love is translated into action long before it is translated into words. At the center of that action is a longing that is frequently misunderstood: **respect.**

Ephesians 5:33 states plainly, "Each one of you also must love his wife as he loves himself, and the wife must respect her husband" (NIV). That instruction has been flattened into cliché in some circles and weaponized in others, but psychologically it reflects something real. While both spouses need love and respect, many men experience respect as the emotional atmosphere in which they can breathe.

Respect communicates belief. It says, *"I trust your judgment." "I value your effort." "I see your strength."* When a man senses that his wife believes in him, something steadies internally. His posture changes. His capacity for tenderness often increases. Confidence and affection are not rivals; they are companions.

Conversely, chronic criticism, especially when public, sarcastic, or dismissive, can strike deeply.

A single correction does not wound a healthy marriage, but patterns do. *Eyerolling*, comparisons to other men, questioning motives in front of others, or framing every decision as incompetence slowly erode dignity. A man who feels small at home will eventually become quiet or defensive. Neither reaction fosters intimacy.

This does not mean wives should suppress disagreement or silence insight. Respect is not the absence of critique; it is the posture in which critique is delivered. One can disagree without humiliating. One can correct without belittling. One can challenge without undermining.

Many husbands also long for admiration. Admiration is not ego-stroking; it is affirmation of identity. When a wife says, *"I'm proud of how you handled that,"* or *"I appreciate the way you protect our family,"* she is not inflating pride, she is reinforcing purpose.

Proverbs 18:21 reminds us that *"Death and life are in the power of the tongue"* (NKJV). Words do not simply describe reality; they shape it. A husband consistently spoken to with dignity often rises into it.

The Desire for Partnership

Beyond respect and admiration, many men desire **partnership.**

Genesis 2:18 describes the woman as *"a helper suitable for him"* (NIV). The Hebrew term *ezer* does not imply subordination. It is used elsewhere in Scripture to describe God as Israel's help. It implies strength aligned with strength. Most men do not want a competitor inside their marriage. They want a teammate. Someone who believes in shared vision. Someone who stands beside rather than against.

When a husband senses that his wife is *"with"* him, even when she disagrees, his resilience strengthens. But when he feels that home is a courtroom where he is perpetually on trial, he may stop inviting her into decisions altogether.

Genesis 2:18 describes the woman as "a helper suitable for him" (NIV). The Hebrew term *ezer* does not imply subordination. It is used elsewhere in Scripture to describe God as Israel's help. It implies strength aligned with strength. Most men do not want a competitor inside their marriage. They want a teammate. Someone who believes in shared vision. Someone who stands beside rather than against. When a husband senses that his wife is "with" him, even when she disagrees, his resilience strengthens. But when he feels that home is a courtroom where he is perpetually on trial, he may stop inviting her into decisions altogether.

The book of *Proverbs* is candid: "Better to live on a corner of the roof than share a house with a quarrelsome wife" (Proverbs 21:9, NIV). That proverb is not a condemnation of women; it is a commentary on climate. Hostility corrodes intimacy. Many men are less afraid of conflict itself than of sustained tension without resolution. If home feels like a space of constant emotional volatility, withdrawal can become a survival strategy.

It is also necessary to speak honestly about sexual desire. For many husbands, sexual intimacy is not compartmentalized from emotional connection. While culture caricatures male desire as purely physical, the reality is often more layered. Sexual closeness can communicate affirmation, acceptance, and belonging. It reassures a husband that he is wanted, not merely tolerated. When physical intimacy is frequent and mutually enjoyable, many men experience increased emotional openness. There is another dimension to what many men want in marriage that is often overlooked because it does not fit easily into emotional language: *significance.*

For many husbands, marriage is not simply companionship; it is purpose intertwined with identity. When a man feels that his efforts matter, that his work contributes meaningfully to the household, that his decisions are trusted, that his leadership is not perpetually second-guessed, he experiences *dignity.* Dignity is stabilizing. It reduces defensiveness. It lowers the instinct to compete. It increases the desire to serve.

Conversely, when a man senses that nothing, he does is enough, that every effort is measured against an invisible standard he cannot reach, he may stop initiating altogether. This is not laziness; it is discouragement. Discouragement slowly erodes motivation. A husband who once pursued energetically can become passive if he believes his pursuit will always fall short.

Respect, then, is not about flattery; it is about recognizing effort. It is about saying, "I see what you carry." Even when improvement is needed, acknowledgment must precede correction. *Scripture* affirms the power of encouragement: "Therefore encourage one another and build each other up" (1 Thessalonians 5:11, NIV).

Building up is not naïve optimism. It is strategic reinforcement of what is good so that it grows stronger.

Men also long for ***clarity.*** Many husbands experience anxiety when relational expectations feel shifting or undefined. When a wife can articulate what makes her feel loved, when she can express needs directly rather than through layered hints, it reduces confusion. Clarity lowers the defensive instinct and increases the likelihood of meaningful change. A man who knows how to succeed is more likely to try.

Underneath the desire for respect, partnership, intimacy, and peace sits a simple longing: to be chosen. Not merely as a provider. Not merely as a co-parent. But as a man. When a wife communicates, through word and affection, "I would still choose you," something deep settles.

When those longings are acknowledged, even imperfectly, many men become softer, more attentive, and more emotionally available. Safety breeds openness.

If many men fear inadequacy, many women fear invisibility.

That fear is rarely articulated in those exact terms. Instead, it shows up in subtler language: "We don't talk anymore." "You're always busy."

"You don't notice me." Beneath those sentences is a longing not merely to be accommodated, but to be emotionally seen. For many wives, emotional presence is not optional in marriage; it is foundational. Without it, everything else—security, intimacy, peace—feels unstable.

Scripture frames a husband's love in strikingly relational language. "Husbands, love your wives, just as Christ loved the church and gave himself up for her" (Ephesians 5:25, NIV). Christ's love is not distant provision alone. It is attentive, sacrificial, and engaged. It listens. It draws near. It moves toward vulnerability rather than away from it. When women read that verse, they do not imagine a stoic provider standing at the edge of the room. They imagine a man whose heart is turned toward them.

Emotional safety is the environment in which many women thrive. Safety means that when she reveals confusion, frustration, or hurt, she is not dismissed as "too emotional" or "overreacting." It means her interior world is not trivialized. When a wife shares something that matters deeply to her, and the response she receives is distraction or impatience, she often experiences more than disappointment. She experiences exposure without covering.

To feel emotionally safe is to know that your words will be handled with care.

In the early stages of marriage, emotional attentiveness is often abundant. Questions are asked. Stories are exchanged. Memories are explored. But familiarity can breed efficiency. Conversations become logistical. Calendars replace curiosity. Functional exchanges crowd out emotional depth.

Many husbands are surprised when their wives express dissatisfaction because, from their perspective, nothing catastrophic has happened. There has been no betrayal, no shouting, no overt cruelty. But emotional neglect is rarely dramatic. It is incremental.

When a woman begins to feel unseen, she may initially increase effort. She may pursue conversation more persistently. She may express her needs more clearly. If those efforts are repeatedly minimized or misread as criticism, she may eventually withdraw emotionally. That withdrawal can be misinterpreted by her husband as moodiness or unpredictability, when in reality it is self-protection.

Another central longing for many women is affection that is not always a prelude to sex. Non-sexual touch, holding hands, sitting close, a hand on her back while walking through a doorway, communicates warmth without expectation. For many wives, such gestures build the emotional safety necessary for deeper intimacy. Without them, physical advances can feel abrupt or disconnected from the relational context she needs to open fully.

Biology reinforces this dynamic. Oxytocin, sometimes referred to as the bonding hormone, is often released through affectionate touch and emotionally meaningful interaction. For many women, desire grows out of connection.

It does not precede it. When connection erodes, desire frequently follows. This does not mean women are less sexual. It means their sexuality is often relationally anchored.

Song of Solomon offers a portrait of marital intimacy that is emotionally and verbally rich. "You have stolen my heart, my sister, my bride; you have stolen my heart with one glance of your eyes" (Song 4:9, NIV). Notice the emphasis on admiration, words, gaze. Many wives crave this kind of attentiveness. They want to feel not only physically desired but emotionally cherished.

Cherishing is different from tolerating. It is different from assuming. It requires intentional notice. It requires verbal affirmation. It requires pursuit.

Pursuit, in marriage, does not mean dramatic romance every week. It means initiative. It means remembering that familiarity does not eliminate the need for intentionality. A wife who feels pursued often relaxes into affection more easily. A wife who feels taken for granted often grows guarded.

Security also plays a significant role. While financial stability can contribute to a sense of safety, relational consistency is often more significant. When a husband's mood fluctuates unpredictably or when he withdraws without explanation, many wives experience subtle anxiety. *Consistency builds trust. Predictability fosters peace.* When she knows that he will respond with patience rather than volatility, she can risk vulnerability more freely.

There is also a spiritual dimension to what many women desire in marriage. Numerous wives carry quiet spiritual burdens, praying for their families, worrying about the future, seeking direction for their children. When a husband engages spiritually, initiating prayer, discussing faith, expressing dependence on God, it often communicates leadership in the deepest sense. It says, "You are not carrying this alone."

When spiritual responsibility rests entirely on one spouse, imbalance can grow. *Partnership in faith deepens emotional intimacy.*

Like men, women also carry unspoken fears. If a husband fears inadequacy, a wife often fears abandonment—not necessarily physical abandonment, but emotional drift. She may wonder, "If I stop asking for connection, will we slowly become strangers?"

That fear can intensify her efforts to draw him near. If he interprets those efforts as nagging rather than longing, both end up wounded.

Understanding this fear reframes conflict. A wife who raises her voice may not be attempting to dominate; she may be attempting to be heard before distance grows wider.

A husband who retreats may not be refusing intimacy; he may be overwhelmed by the emotional intensity and unsure how to repair it.

When men and women interpret one another's behaviors through fear rather than empathy, cycles form quickly. She pursues harder. He withdraws further. She escalates. He shuts down. Neither recognizes that beneath the surface, both are reaching for connection in the only way they know how.

What a woman wants, then, is layered but coherent. She wants emotional presence that feels engaged rather than distracted. She wants affection that is warm rather than transactional. She wants verbal affirmation that acknowledges her value. She wants security rooted in consistency. She wants spiritual partnership that shares responsibility.

When these longings are met, even imperfectly, many wives soften. Criticism decreases. Affection increases. Sexual openness often grows. Peace becomes more sustainable.

The irony of marriage is that men and women often want the same outcome—closeness, affirmation, safety—but approach it from different angles. He may move toward physical intimacy seeking reassurance.

She may move toward conversation seeking reassurance. When each learns to meet the other at the point of longing rather than the point of irritation, connection strengthens.

Marriage thrives not when difference disappears, but when difference is interpreted generously.

What a man wants and what a woman wants are not opposing agendas. They are complementary longings expressed through different emotional dialects. He wants respect, affirmation, and reassurance that he is enough. She wants emotional presence, affection, and reassurance that she is seen. Both want to feel chosen. Both want to feel safe.

Most marital leaks do not begin with hatred. They begin with misinterpretation.

When a wife complains about distance, she may be asking for closeness. When a husband withdraws after criticism, he may be protecting dignity. When sexual desire feels mismatched, it may reflect unmet emotional needs on both sides rather than selfishness on one.

Understanding does not erase differences. *It dignifies it.* And dignity changes tone.

When a husband begins to speak in ways that build emotional safety, many wives soften. When a wife begins to communicate respect and belief in her husband, many men become more attentive. What felt like tension becomes synergy.

Marriage begins to seal.

Drip-Free Practice

This week, do not guess. Ask your spouse directly:

"What makes you feel most respected?"

"What makes you feel most cherished?"

Listen without defending. Clarify without interrupting.

Then choose one specific adjustment and practice it consistently.

Do not aim for transformation in a day. Aim for faithfulness in small changes. Leaks are sealed one repair at a time.

Reflection

Before pointing outward, look inward.

1. Where have I been loving from my own preference rather than my spouse's need?

2. Where have I assumed motives instead of asking questions?

3. Where have I allowed frustration to replace curiosity?

"Through wisdom a house is built, and by understanding it is established" (Proverbs 24:3, NKJV).

Understanding begins with humility.

Application

Set aside one uninterrupted hour this week — without phones, without television, without distraction.

Complete these sentences together:

- "I feel most loved when…"
- "I feel most respected when…"
- "I feel most distant when…"

Do not debate responses. Simply receive them. Write down what you learn. Review it monthly. Let it guide how you show up.

Prayer

Lord, teach me how my spouse experiences love. Where I have assumed, give me patience. Where I have reacted, give me understanding. Where pride has hardened me, soften me. Help me love not only with sincerity, but with accuracy. Seal the leaks created by misunderstanding and strengthen the bond we share. Amen.

Affirmation

We choose to understand before we accuse. We choose to respect before we react. We choose to cherish before we criticize. Our love will not leak through assumption. It will be strengthened through understanding.

***

Understanding what a man wants and what a woman wants brings clarity, but clarity alone does not sustain warmth. Even when love is translated correctly, it can grow predictable.

Covenant requires more than accuracy; it requires intention. When routine replaces delight, connection slowly loses its flavor.

***

Chapter 6

Marriage Spices

***

For all the sermons preached on marriage, one book of the Bible remains curiously underexplored in the pulpit: *Song of Songs* (also called *Song of Solomon*). It is a book overflowing with gardens, fragrances, orchards, spices, kisses, touches, vineyards, and delight. It is poetry, and it is passion. It is devotion, and it is desire. It is a covenant, and it is chemistry. It is scripture's most unapologetic declaration that marriage is meant to be flavorful.

The Flavor of Marriage: Alive and Engaged

The imagery of *Song of Songs* is not accidental. It is agricultural and sensory for a reason. Love is described as wine, gardens, lilies, apple trees, fountains, myrrh, cinnamon, aloes, saffron, pomegranates, sweet fruit, and sacred oils. The marriage portrayed in its pages is not bland, sterile, or mechanical. It is fragrant. It is flavorful. It is alive. The senses are engaged. The body is honored. Desire is celebrated, not shamed. Covenant becomes a garden tended, not a contract endured.

Some marriages lose this flavor over time, not because the couple no longer loves each other, but because the marriage has lost its spice. The busy years come—the roof leaks. The children grow. The ministry demands. The house needs repairs—the laundry multiplies. The inbox fills. The fatigue expands. And somewhere along the way, the marriage becomes more about function than fragrance. Rooms once filled with delight become occupied by duty. Bedrooms once filled with pursuit become places of collapse. Silence replaces curiosity. Routine replaces romance. Touch becomes optional. Humor becomes rare. And both spouses quietly wonder where the flavor went. But marriage was never designed to survive on duty alone. Duty sustains commitment. Flavor sustains covenant.

When God created Adam and Eve, He did not place them in a sterile environment. He placed them in a garden, a rich, sensory world full of color, fragrance, texture, sound, and taste. Eden was not a cubicle. It was an orchard. In Hebrew imagination, gardens represent delight, abundance, and intimacy. The garden was not merely where marriage began; it was how marriage was meant to feel.

Why Does Marriage Lose Its Spice?

Scripture never reduces marriage to paperwork, duty, or mere survival. When Proverbs celebrates marriage, it describes delight and satisfaction (Proverbs 5:18–19, NIV).

When Paul speaks of marriage, he calls it a mystery that reveals Christ and the church (Ephesians 5:32, NIV). When the prophets speak of covenant, they use the language of love, pursuit, longing, and faithfulness. When Jesus performs His first miracle, He does it at a wedding feast full of wine and celebration. Heaven's final event in Revelation is not a courtroom or a lecture hall; it is a wedding banquet. Scripture opens with a marriage and ends with a marriage. God seems to enjoy weddings and everything they represent.

If God intended marriage to be a banquet, a vineyard, an orchard, and a garden, why do so many couples settle for bowls of plain rice and unsalted crackers spiritually, emotionally, and sexually? Some do so because no one taught them the language of intimacy. Some do so because shame silenced desire. Some do so because they never saw spice at home growing up. Others, because they experienced spice without covenant, now fear the collision of the two. And still others because life has worn them thin.

But here is the truth: marriage without flavor becomes brittle. Brittleness leads to boredom.

Boredom leads to curiosity elsewhere. Curiosity elsewhere leads to distraction, and distraction becomes its own drip. Not every affair begins with lust. Many begin with lack: lack of attention, lack of celebration, lack of novelty, lack of play, lack of spice.

Marriage needs not only love but seasoning. Seasoning is what turns ingredients into meals. Two people can share a mortgage, a ministry, a schedule, and a bed, and still not be sharing a life rich in flavor. Marriage thrives on spice, on warmth, on surprise, on pursuit, on delight, on sensuality, on affection, on laughter, on vulnerability, on hospitality of heart and body.

Spice: Worship with the Body

Theologians often point out that *the Song of Songs* never once mentions God directly, and yet the entire book is drenched in holiness because it honors what God created. It is a reminder that delight is not secular and desire is not wicked. Pleasure is not the devil's invention. Desire, when expressed by covenant, is worship with the body. Unholy desire is desire without covenant. Holy desire is desire expressed within a covenant.

Spices of a Flavorful Marriage

A flavorful marriage engages all the senses; touch, taste, sight, scent, sound, and does so without shame.

When marriages neglect the senses, intimacy dries up. When marriages cultivate the senses, intimacy ripens. Spice makes marriage memorable. Spice makes marriage magnetic. Spice makes marriage sustainable.

Some marriages need a miracle. Others simply need seasoning.

Every spice reveals a dimension of intimacy; emotional, relational, and yes, sexual. Spices awaken the senses. Spices stir memory. Spices create anticipation. Spices transform ordinary ingredients into extraordinary meals. Marriage works the same way. Love is the ingredient; intimacy is the seasoning. When a marriage is seasoned well, affection flows without force, desire arises without shame, and covenant becomes delightful instead of dutiful.

Below are six spices frequently associated with love and covenant in Scripture, particularly in *the Song of Songs* (also called *Song of Solomon*). These spices provide a language for understanding the many flavors a marriage needs to remain alive and engaging.

Cinnamon: Warmth & Affection

Cinnamon adds warmth. Its fragrance fills the room quickly, and its taste lingers. In marriage, warmth is communicated through affection, touch, tone, attention, and presence.

Warmth is often the first spice to fade when marriage becomes transactional or exhausting. A cold marriage is not always hateful; sometimes it is simply unattended.

Warmth shows up in small gestures: an arm around a shoulder during prayer, a hand placed gently on the lower back in public, a kiss on the forehead before bed, laughter at the end of a long day, or a spouse making the other's drink *"the way they like it."* These micro-affections are the cinnamon sticks of marriage; they diffuse comfort into the atmosphere. Warmth also has a sensual dimension. *Song of Songs* says,

"His left hand is under my head, and his right hand embraces me..." (Song of Songs 2:6, AMP) This is an affectionate embrace, not merely a sexual one. Physical affection outside the bedroom is often the bridge that leads couples into sexual intimacy within the bedroom. Many women need warming before they need romance; many men interpret warming as romance. *Warmth makes both possible.*

When warmth disappears, spouses stop reaching. Touch becomes functional (passing items, handing dishes) instead of affectionate. Over time, the absence of warmth becomes the presence of distance.

Saffron: Extravagance & Sacred Indulgence

Saffron was one of the most expensive spices in the ancient world. It symbolized indulgence, luxury, and intentional investment. In marriage, saffron represents those moments where couples choose to be extravagant with one another, not financially extravagant, but emotionally and relationally extravagant.

Extravagance sounds like:

- *"Let's slow down."*
- *"Let's make this special."*
- *"Let's celebrate this milestone."*
- *"Let's dress up for each other."*
- *"Let's linger a little longer."*

Saffron is the spice that refuses to treat marriage as routine. It insists that love deserves ceremony. Couples who practice saffron plan dates, take trips, create rituals, and mark anniversaries. Rituals matter more than people admit. Ritual turns affection into memory. Saffron also carries a sexual dimension. *Song of Songs* describes the bride as a garden containing saffron (*Song of Songs 4:13–14*), suggesting indulgence and delight. Sexual intimacy that is unhurried and attentive, where spouses become students of each other's pleasure, is saffron in action. It is indulgent without guilt. Holy without stiffness. Playful without shame.

Myrrh: Passion, Suffering & Desire

Myrrh is a bittersweet spice. It was used for anointing, worship, healing, and preparation for burial.

Myrrh represents the complexity of love, its passion, its sacrifice, and its endurance. Marriage is not all sweetness. Love requires dying to pride, forgiving offenses, and choosing pursuit even when tired. *Song of Songs* uses myrrh in profoundly sensual ways:

"My beloved is to me a sachet of myrrh resting between my breasts." (Song of Songs 1:13, NIV) This is not just poetic, it is erotic. Myrrh here symbolizes arousal and nearness. Passion requires proximity. You cannot pursue from across the room. You cannot ignite desire through indifference. *Passion needs presence.*

Myrrh also represents suffering well. There are seasons when love hurts—crisis, illness, ministry demand, financial stress, infertility, aging, grief. Myrrh reminds the couple that some parts of love require endurance. Passion without sacrifice is lust. Sacrifice without passion is martyrdom. Marriage needs both.

Aloes: Refreshment & Joy

Aloes are cooling, soothing, and refreshing. They restore after heat. In marriage, aloes represent joy, humor, and the ability to recover. Many marriages suffer not because of sin or betrayal, but because they forget how to laugh. Humor ventilates tension. Joy resets the emotional climate. Play keeps marriages young.

Aloes show up sensually as well. Refreshment in the bedroom often comes from novelty, curiosity, and experimentation within covenant boundaries. Couples who refuse to become predictable in their intimacy find that desire ages well. There is nothing sinful about married lovers surprising each other.

A refreshed marriage is one where joy has not been suffocated by responsibility. Ministry couples often lose this spice fastest, serving God publicly while suffering privately, because joy became optional.

Calamus: Playfulness & Surprise

Calamus has a sweet fragrance and was used to make perfume and oil. It represents playfulness, flirtation, and delightful surprise. Many spouses are faithful but not playful. Faithfulness keeps the covenant intact. Playfulness keeps the covenant enjoyable.

Playfulness is present when couples flirt with each other, send small messages during the day, whisper private jokes, dance in the kitchen, or steal kisses in passing. Playfulness keeps romance light. It breaks the ice when life becomes heavy. It reminds spouses that marriage is not merely a ministry assignment; it is a delight.

Calamus expresses itself sexually, too. Playful lovers have better intimate outcomes because they are not afraid to laugh, adjust, and discover. *Playfulness removes pressure and invites curiosity, two essential ingredients for desire.*

Nard: Value, Fragrance & Erotic Honor

Nard was rare and costly. In the ancient world, it had to be harvested from the base of the Himalayas, transported across borders, and purchased at great expense. To possess nard was to possess something worthy of kings, weddings, and sacred moments. Because of this, Nard represents value in marriage, the affirmation that your spouse is not merely familiar, but priceless.

Song of Songs says,

"While the king was at his table, my perfume spread its fragrance." (Song of Songs 1:12, NIV) The perfume referenced is nard. It is not worn for neighbors or strangers but for the beloved.

Nard fills the room. It changes the air. Desire becomes atmospheric. Honor becomes sensual. Nard communicates, *"I prepared for you."*

This preparation leads to a second dimension of nard: fragrance. Fragrance lingers. It precedes. It enters the room before you speak. It remains after you depart. Fragrance in marriage is the equivalent of relational atmosphere; the emotional climate couples create for each other. Honor is the fragrance of love.

Disrespect is the odor of contempt. Couples who fail to steward atmosphere sabotage intimacy before it begins.

The atmosphere also affects the bedroom. Few people experience sexual desire in climates filled with criticism, anger, sarcasm, or neglect. Nard teaches us that desire must be honored before it is awakened.

Honor is foreplay. Atmosphere is foreplay. Softness of tone is foreplay. Affirmation is foreplay. Preparation is foreplay. Song of Songs reveals that desire is not mechanical; it is cultivated.

Nard also carries a third dimension: erotic anointing. In the ancient Near East, oils were used to prepare bodies and beds for intimacy. Nard was part of perfumed oils used for bridal nights. It signified readiness, attention, and celebration of the marital union.

Erotic honor says, *"I present myself to you with care."* This is not vanity; it is covenantal hospitality of the body.

Modern marriage often loses nard, not because spouses stop loving each other, but because they stop valuing each other. Value leaks through familiarity, fatigue, assumptions, and entitlement. Lovers become co-managers of children, bills, projects, and ministry. Honor evaporates under the weight of efficiency. Desire dies in climates where value is absent.

When a husband honors his wife with words, with attention, with sexual desire, with spiritual covering, and with responsiveness, nard fills the room. When a wife honors her husband with admiration, respect, pursuit, affirmation, and erotic generosity, nard fills the room.

Nard is the spice that turns lovers into treasures, not roommates. It whispers, "You are not merely convenient; you are chosen."

Each spice reveals a doorway into intimacy.

Some couples have warmth but no surprise. Others have passion but no joy. Others have indulgence but no honor. Others have playfulness but no sacrifice. Marriage was designed to have them all.

When flavor is lost, it does not return to a marriage by accident. Gardens do not bloom because of hope alone. Vineyards do not produce wine without cultivation. Spice does not infuse without heat, time, and attention. If marriage is a sensory ecosystem, as Scripture suggests, then restoration requires intention.

Couples often assume that flavor should be automatic if love is present. But flavor in marriage behaves more like fragrance in perfume: *it must be distilled, applied, refreshed, and sometimes rediscovered.* Spices do not shout; they reveal themselves to those who taste. If a marriage has become bland, predictable, or dry, it is not always because something is wrong. Sometimes it is because nothing has been intentionally made right. Most couples do not lose flavor through adultery, violence, or betrayal. They lose flavor through fatigue, complacency, distraction, and assumption.

Here are five practices that help restore flavor to marriages that have settled into neutral

1. Reignite Pursuit on Both Sides

Pursuit is often the first casualty in long-term relationships. Many spouses assume that because they "have" each other, they no longer need to "win" each other. But the covenant did not kill pursuit; marriage simply made pursuit holy. Pursuit has emotional and sexual layers.

Emotionally, pursuit sounds like:

- *"Tell me what's been on your mind lately."*
- *"I want to understand you better."*
- *"I'm still curious about you."*

Sexually, pursuit sounds like:

- *"I desire you."*

- *"You're beautiful."*
- *"I want to make time for us tonight."*

Pursuit is not pressure; it is an invitation. *Song of Songs* shows the pursuit of both spouses. The beloved says, *"Let my beloved come into his garden..."* (Song of Songs 4:16, NIV), and the lover responds with movement and desire. Pursuit is mutual, not male-only.

2. Engage the Senses Again

Every spice is sensory. Every marriage needs sensory revival. To reawaken the senses, couples must move beyond thinking and enter embodied connection:

- *Sight* (beauty, preparation, presentation)
- *Sound* (tone, laughter, affirmation)
- *Touch* (non-sexual and sexual affection)
- *Smell* (fragrance, environment, atmosphere)
- *Taste* (shared meals, kisses, indulgences)

Many marriages suffer because spouses live only in their minds, not their bodies. But the body is part of the covenant. *You cannot kiss with your doctrine. You cannot hug with your theology. You cannot make love with your beliefs.* Beliefs must become embodied to become intimacy.

Sensory engagement is not secular; it is sacred. Sensuality is not sinful; it is biblical. God created senses before sin entered the world.

3. Create Rhythms of Delight

Delight does not survive on spontaneity alone. It must be scheduled, cultivated, and protected. Couples who prioritize delight find that fatigue loses its power and bitterness loses its territory.

Rhythms of delight include:

- *Weekly date nights* (even inexpensive ones)
- *Surprise gestures*
- *Private rituals* (inside jokes, favorite spots, shared hobbies)
- *Celebration of milestones*
- *Vacations and getaways*
- *Sabbath-style rest*

Delight is also sensual. Long, unhurried physical intimacy. Touch without agenda. Kissing is not a prelude but a language. Time in the bedroom that is not rushed between chores and exhaustion. Delight demands margin.

4. Practice Play Without Shame

Play is the missing ingredient in many Christian marriages. Responsibility becomes so heavy that couples forget how to be light. But play keeps intimacy young and desire curious.

Play looks like:

1. *Flirting again*
2. *Dancing in the kitchen*
3. *Chasing each other through the house*
4. *Sending messages during the day*
5. *Wearing something attractive for your spouse*
6. *Trying new things in the bedroom*
7. *Laughing in the middle of lovemaking when something goes sideways*

Shame kills play. So does self-consciousness. Lovers who refuse to play become performers. Lovers who play become partners.

5. Rebuild Sacred Touch

Touch is the language of the body. It communicates comfort, attention, attraction, and desire. Many couples experience a decline in touch that has nothing to do with conflict and everything to do with pace. When touch disappears, the marriage begins to starve. Three dimensions of touch must be rebuilt:

- *Non-Sexual Touch* — holding hands, hugs, forehead kisses, strokes, proximity
- *Affectionate Sexual Touch* — sensual contact without the pressure of intercourse
- *Erotic Touch* — pleasurable contact that awakens desire and satisfaction

Song of Songs integrates all three, without embarrassment and without apology. Sacred touch is not pornographic. Porn takes without covenant. Scripture is given within the covenant. When flavor returns to marriage, desire awakens naturally. And when desire awakens, union deepens. Sexual intimacy stops feeling like a duty or an obligation and becomes an expression of delight, honor, and curiosity. The bedroom becomes the sanctuary, not the courtroom.

Drip-Free Practice

Choose one spice to reintroduce into your marriage this week intentionally. Do not announce it as a project; embody it as a gift. *Warmth. Extravagance. Passion. Joy. Playfulness. Honor.* Let the spice do the talking. Flavor teaches faster than lectures.

Reflection Questions

1. Which spice has always been natural for you in marriage, and which has faded over time?

2. What sensory aspects of your marriage need revival—touch, taste, scent, sound, or sight?

3. How did your upbringing or church culture shape your comfort or discomfort with sensuality in covenant?

Application Exercise

Plan one flavor experience with your spouse within the next seven days. It can be a date, a meal, an atmosphere, a surprise, a playful encounter, or an unhurried evening of intimacy. The goal is not performance. The goal is delight.

Prayer

Father, thank You for creating marriage to be delightful, flavorful, and holy. Restore warmth where there is coldness, passion where there is fatigue, joy where there is heaviness, and honor where there has been neglect.

Teach us to pursue one another again, with affection, curiosity, and grace. May our marriage be a garden that You plant, water, and bless. Amen.

Affirmation

Our marriage is designed for flavor, delight, and covenant joy. We will pursue one another with honor, playfulness, and intention.

***

Flavor deepens intimacy, but intimacy is shaped long before marriage begins. Every husband and wife enters a covenant already formed by family, culture, church, silence, shame, and experience. Before sexual intimacy can flourish, what formed it must be understood. Desire does not begin on the wedding night; it carries a history.

***

Chapter 7

Redeeming Sexual Formation

***

"Adam and his wife were both naked, and they felt no shame." (Genesis 2:25, NIV)

"Pleasure is not a corruption of holiness, but a partner of covenant." Gregory of Nyssa

Before marriage carried disappointments, before desire was tangled in fear, before comparison robbed affection, before bodies became battlegrounds for insecurity, there was a garden. And in that garden, there were two lovers, naked, unashamed, unafraid, unhidden. They did not apologize for their desire. They did not justify their pleasure. They did not negotiate their belonging. They did not perform intimacy. They received it.

The first gift God gave humanity was not command or instruction, but communion. Communion with Himself, communion with creation, and communion with one another. Before they prayed together, Adam and Eve delighted together.

Before they worshiped with words, they worshiped with their bodies. Before they built altars, they built affection. God planted a garden, and in that garden, He placed desire. Not the counterfeit desire that consumes without covenant, but sacred desire that gives and receives with joy.

When Scripture tells us they were "*naked and unashamed,*" it is not offering trivia about ancient fashion. It is describing a condition of the soul. Shame had not yet arrived to police desire. Sin had not yet arrived to corrupt delight. Trauma had not yet arrived to make touch unsafe. Disappointment had not yet arrived to make affection guarded. Anxiety had not yet arrived to tighten the nervous system. They were naked, and their nakedness was not a problem to solve but a glory to behold.

The body was not yet a threat. The body was not yet compared. The body was not yet hidden. The body was not yet weaponized. The body was a temple before it was temptation. Pleasure was liturgy before it became liability. The marriage bed was sacramental before it became secretive. Desire was part of discipleship before discipleship was fragmented from desire.

In Eden, intimacy required no performance because fear was absent. Fear always demands performance. Fear asks, "Am I enough?" Fear asks, "Will you stay?" Fear asks, "Will you compare me?" Fear asks,

"Will you reject me?" In the garden, fear had no voice. Union did not require self-defense. Vulnerability did not require courage. Transparency was effortless. Delight was natural. Communion was embodied.

When the Fall entered the story, the first instinct was not lust. It was hiding. The tragedy was not that bodies became desirable, but that bodies became feared. They covered themselves not because nakedness was sinful, but because nakedness was now dangerous. What was once communion became exposure. What was once delight became self-protection. What was once worship became worry. Shame arrived before lust ever did.

And we have lived east of Eden ever since, desiring communion, fearing exposure, longing for touch, anticipating rejection, hungry for delight, bracing for disappointment. We still dream of nakedness without shame, but we build marriages clothed in self-defense. We hide behind busyness, behind silence, behind theological language that sanitizes desire, behind religious performance that divorces holiness from pleasure. We have sanctuaries for worship but not for delight. We have liturgies for communion but not for climax. We have theology for the soul but not for the body.

Yet Scripture refuses to surrender the body to shame. The God who clothed Adam and Eve after the Fall did not clothe them to erase desire, but to protect dignity. And the God who became flesh in Jesus Christ did not come to rescue souls from bodies, but to restore bodies to belonging. Redemption does not merely save sinners. Redemption restores lovers. The gospel does not merely prepare us for heaven. It prepares us for communion.

Marriage is meant to be the workshop of this redemption. Not the theater of performance. Not the battlefield of insecurity. Not the laboratory of disappointment. But the place where hiding ends and communion begins again. A SucSEXful marriage does not begin with technique. It begins with theology. If you do not know what intimacy was before the Fall, you will never understand what intimacy is being redeemed into after the cross.

Formation Before the Altar

Sexual formation does not begin in marriage. It begins long before it. It is shaped by family, culture, church, secrecy, silence, trauma, expectation, and comparison. By the time two believers stand at an altar and say, "I do," they are not beginning their sexual story. They are revealing the sexual stories they have already lived.

What is now commonly referred to as purity culture emerged with the aim of protecting Christian young people from sexual sin. Yet for many, it framed desire as dangerous rather than something to be formed, guided, and redeemed. Desire was framed as dangerous. Bodies were framed as stumbling blocks. Sexual attraction was presented as a threat rather than a gift. The emphasis was often abstinence without erotic discipleship, which creates virgins without sexual maturity.

Abstinence is not the same as formation. One can abstain from sexual activity and still be sexually malformed. You can keep your body out of someone's bed and still place your mind in the bondage of shame. *Purity* culture taught restraint but often failed to teach embodiment, consent, curiosity, covenantal pursuit, or pleasure as worship. It taught how to say "no" to sex but rarely taught how to say *"yes"* to intimacy.

Alongside this religious formation came a secular counter-formation. For many believers, pornography became the forbidden classroom of sexual literacy. Pornography trains the mind to pursue pleasure without responsibility, climax without communion, and bodies without personhood. It scripts sex as performance rather than presence, consumption rather than covenant, conquest rather than communion. It teaches that the body is for taking, not for giving. It shapes desire but divorces it from love.

Between purity culture and pornography culture, a generation learned that sex is either too sacred to speak about or too casual to take seriously. In both systems, no one is taught how to disciple desire. No one is taught how to welcome pleasure with holiness. No one is taught how to bless their spouse's body without shame. No one is taught how to integrate faith and arousal. Silence became the unofficial curriculum of Christian sexual formation.

But marriage does not erase these formations. It exposes them. The altar does not reset the nervous system. Wedding vows do not dissolve shame. Sexual ignorance does not become sexual fluency simply because covenant is spoken. The body remembers its formation. The nervous system remembers who it had to become in order to survive adolescence, dating, secrecy, and desire.

Inside marriage, purity culture often reappears as reluctance, fear of initiation, anxiety about nakedness, difficulty with arousal, or guilt about pleasure. Pornographic formation often reappears as performance pressure, comparison fantasies, disappointment in a spouse's body, desire asymmetry, or climax without intimacy. Religious silence becomes marital silence. Shame becomes withdrawal. Secrecy becomes self-protection.

The tragic irony is that marriage becomes the place where believers finally have permission for pleasure, yet there is no formation for how to receive it. Many Christian couples discover they were well discipled in abstinence but never discipled in erotic communion.

They learned how to avoid sexual sin but never learned how to cultivate sexual joy. They preserved virginity but sacrificed curiosity. They maintained modesty but lost embodiment.

Once you see it, the thread is obvious. What was formed in secrecy emerges in covenant. What was disciplined in adolescence surfaces in adulthood. What was suppressed in youth becomes strained in marriage. What was punished becomes performed. What was feared becomes negotiated. What was trained in shame becomes enacted in silence.

Marriage does not create sexual dysfunction. It merely reveals the sexual formation that preceded it. And revelation, though painful, is grace. Healing cannot begin where hiding continues. God does not expose formation to condemn His children but to redeem His lovers. Covenant invites the believer not back into Eden's innocence but into Eden's communion.

These layers of sexual formation do not disappear at the altar. Marriage does not erase the stories we lived before we entered it. Marriage simply gives those stories a partner. For many Christian couples, the wedding day becomes the moment when two sexual histories meet, collide, or finally become visible. What was once private becomes shared. What was once secret becomes known. What was once theoretical becomes embodied.

Without intentional discipleship of desire, couples soon discover that they were never prepared for the sexual world they were expected to inhabit.

This is where many marriages begin to struggle. Not because they lack love or commitment, but because they lack formation. Sexual desire is a powerful force, but desire without guidance becomes anxiety, and anxiety without language becomes silence. Silence in the marriage bed is not neutrality. It is abandonment. When couples cannot name their fears, wounds, frustrations, or hopes, their bodies are left to carry burdens their words were meant to share.

And so, the marriage bed becomes a meeting place for unspoken stories. Shame that never healed. Desire that never matured. Questions that were never answered. Wounds that were never witnessed. Without a framework for covenantal intimacy, couples often revert to coping strategies such as avoidance, performance, endurance, comparison, or withdrawal. These are not failures of morality. They are failures of formation.

Sexual formation must be redeemed. Every believer enters marriage with a sexual formation long before they enter a bedroom. Formation does not begin with wedding vows. It begins in childhood, adolescence, culture, media, and the unspoken rules of our homes and churches.

We learn about sex not only from what was said but from what was never said. Silence catechizes the heart as powerfully as instruction.

For some, desire was framed as dangerous. For others, it was treated as a joke. For others still, it was awakened prematurely through exposure or violation. All of this arrives in the marriage bed unexamined, unnamed, and often misunderstood.

Scripture's first mention of marital intimacy is breathtakingly simple: *"naked and unashamed"* (Genesis 2:25, NIV). This is not naïveté. It is theological anthropology. In God's original design, sexuality is both embodied and innocent, both pleasurable and unashamed, both relational and spiritual. It belongs to covenant, not secrecy. It belongs to delight, not fear.

Between Eden and our modern world lies the distortion of shame. After the Fall, the first instinct was not lust but hiding. First from God, then from one another. They covered their bodies not because bodies became sinful, but because bodies became vulnerable.

Modern couples often assume they are struggling because they are incompatible, unromantic, or insufficiently spiritual. In reality, most are wrestling with unredeemed formation. Their bodies inherited stories they never consciously chose.

Their nervous systems learned patterns long before their spirits learned theology. Marriage does not erase these patterns. Marriage reveals them.

Many believers enter marriage thinking sexual intimacy is primarily biological. But sex is also theological, psychological, and narrative. Bodies remember what minds try to forget. Desire is shaped by attention, rejection, affection, safety, and fear. A person can love God passionately and serve Him faithfully while still carrying a sexual formation never touched by healing grace.

To redeem sexual intimacy in marriage, we must first redeem sexual formation in the believer. Two dominant narratives shape the sexual imagination of our age: purity culture and pornography culture. Though seemingly opposite, both distort desire and leave the marriage bed impoverished. Purity culture teaches fear of desire. Pornography teaches consumption of desire. One suppresses. The other exploits. Both malform.

Many of today's Christian adults graduated from purity culture as adolescents and entered pornography culture as adults, starved by one, overstimulated by the other, and discipled by neither into covenant.

Purity culture often emphasized behavioral avoidance such as "do not touch," "do not awaken," and "do not engage," without teaching the goodness of desire, the beauty of pleasure, the dignity of bodies, or the covenantal purpose of intimacy. Young Christians were told to *wait*, *save themselves*, and *stay pure*, but were rarely taught what they were saving themselves for. Desire became conflated with sin. Lust became confused with attraction. Pleasure became implied as dangerous rather than as the prelude to covenant joy.

Pornography then entered the gap left by silence. Porn disciples the body into a sexuality without covenant, patience, exclusivity, tenderness, or rest. It teaches stimulation without intimacy, novelty without commitment, climax without affection, and pleasure without personhood. It disconnects sex from union and turns bodies into objects of consumption.

The tragedy is that purity starved formation while pornography distorted it. Neither taught delight. Neither taught covenant. Neither taught tenderness. Neither taught how to pursue pleasure without shame. Redeeming formation requires neither the rigidity of purity panic nor the indulgence of pornographic imitation. It requires something Edenic. Nakedness without shame. Pleasure without secrecy. Desire without condemnation. Covenant without fear.

Not all sexual difficulty in marriage arises from moral formation. Some arise from trauma, and trauma does not need to be dramatic to be formative. Trauma can include childhood exposure to sexual content before the mind was prepared, coercion, pressure, ridicule, betrayal, unwanted touch, or any experience that overwhelms the nervous system's capacity to process.

Trauma does not merely reside in memory. It resides in physiology. The nervous system is built to prioritize survival over pleasure. When the body perceives danger, real or remembered, it tightens, withdraws, dissociates, or numbs. A spouse may intellectually desire closeness while physically shutting down. This is not rebellion. It is protection.

When the body has learned to survive, it must later learn how to receive. Many trauma survivors struggle to understand why they can be aroused in theory but disconnected in practice. A wife may long for closeness but find her pelvis involuntarily tense. A husband may desire his wife deeply but mentally disappear during intimacy. Their bodies are not betraying them. Their bodies are shielding them.

The gospel speaks not only to the soul but also to the nervous system. Jesus restores bodies as well as spirits. He touches without violating. He heals without rushing. He dignifies what shame has humiliated.

Trauma healing in marriage requires slowness, safety, curiosity, and consent. It requires the spouse to become not a savior but a sanctuary. Pleasure becomes possible when the nervous system no longer anticipates pain. When a traumatized spouse experiences pleasure without fear for the first time, it is more than arousal. It is resurrection. It is the nervous system learning that touch can be safe again.

Redeeming Desire in Covenant

Desire is not only biological; it is also learned. Every believer carries *desire scripts* written by family culture, media, faith communities, and personal experience. Some learned that desire is dangerous and must be suppressed. Others learned that desire is functional, existing for reproduction or marital duty. Others learned that desire is performative, something to display for affirmation or validation. These scripts show up in the marriage bed long before couples have language for them.

A man raised to believe his sexuality is a threat may enter marriage *apologizing* for his desire. A woman raised to believe her sexuality is a temptation to men may enter marriage, *withholding* hers. These scripts are not evidence of incompatibility but evidence of formation. Before lovers can learn how to touch one another, they must learn how to narrate their stories.

Before they can receive pleasure, they must *believe* they are allowed to. Before they can offer pleasure, they must know what delights the other.

Shame is one of the primary enemies of covenant intimacy. Shame says, *"Hide. Do not reveal. Do not ask. Do not want."* Shame is not modesty; shame is muteness. It steals the language of desire and replaces it with fear. A spouse who cannot name desire cannot guide their lover toward pleasure. A spouse who cannot name discomfort cannot guide their lover away from pain. Silence becomes the enemy of intimacy.

Shame often wears spiritual clothing. A husband may say he does not want to *"burden"* his wife with desire, but beneath the language lies the fear of rejection. A wife may say she does not want to *"be selfish,"* but beneath the modesty lies the fear of being seen. Shame disguises itself as virtue, but Scripture never treats delight as sin. The lovers of Song of Songs declare, *"Eat, friends, drink, and drink your fill of love!"* (Song 5:1, NIV). This is not hesitant language; it is celebratory. Scripture does not apologize for covenant pleasure; it blesses it.

When pleasure is blessed, shame begins to lose its authority. A believer cannot enjoy their body if they secretly believe God merely tolerates it.

If the body is a temple, then pleasure within covenant is not indulgence; it is *holy enjoyment* of what God declared good. To redeem sexual formation, we must recover blessing.

Christian couples often assume passion will return through spontaneity, novelty, or frequency. But eroticism is not sustained by novelty alone; it is sustained by *safety*. A spouse cannot surrender to pleasure if they are bracing for criticism. They cannot relax into arousal if they are negotiating insecurity. They cannot climax if their nervous system is monitoring danger. Safety is not boring; safety is erotic. When the heart feels held, the body feels free.

Safety takes many forms: consistent affection, gentle tone, attentive presence, nonjudgmental curiosity, patience, and protection from ridicule. These are not *"soft skills"* of marriage; they are erotic competencies. The nervous system has two primary modes when approaching intimacy: protection or participation. Protection shuts down desire. Participation opens it. When lovers begin to see safety as erotic, they discover that desire was not fragile; it was simply waiting for *permission*.

This redefines foreplay. Foreplay is not merely what happens minutes before penetration. Foreplay is the tone of the marriage. Foreplay is how spouses speak to one another, how they pursue one another, how they attend to one another, and how they allow one another to rest. When foreplay becomes a lifestyle rather than a sequence, the body learns to remain open.

Curiosity is one of the most underdeveloped virtues in Christian intimacy. Anxiety guesses. Curiosity asks. Guessing leads to assumptions. Assumptions lead to disappointment. Discovery requires curiosity. Lovers are not born; lovers are learned. To be a lover is to become a student of the other, of their story, body, rhythms, delight, and wounds.

Permission is tied to curiosity. Many believers have never permitted themselves to *want*, to *ask*, to *initiate*, or to *enjoy*. They approach intimacy as an obligation or a duty, not as exploration or worship. Permission reframes sex from marital duty to marital delight. It reframes pleasure from indulgence to inheritance. It reframes eroticism from threat to covenant.

Paul writes, *"The husband should fulfill his marital duty to his wife, and likewise the wife to her husband"* (1 Corinthians 7:3, NIV). Duty in Paul's language is not drudgery; it is *mutual devotion*. Mutual devotion implies mutual delight. Pleasure is not selfishness; it is part of the economy of giving and receiving. Curiosity and permission dismantle pressure, and pleasure cannot thrive under pressure.

Many couples are spiritually mature and sexually inexperienced. They know how to pray together, serve together, fast together, and intercede together, but they do not know how to please one another. This is not hypocrisy; it is compartmentalization.

The Church has discipled the soul but often neglected the body. It taught restraint but rarely taught delight. Spiritual formation without sexual formation produces holy people who feel sexually disoriented. They know how to worship God but not how to receive pleasure without guilt. They know how to pursue righteousness but not how to pursue one another with abandonment. They know how to give sacrificially but not how to receive with joy.

The solution is not less spirituality but more integration. Paul does not treat the body as something to escape but as something to offer: *"Present your bodies as a living sacrifice"* (Romans 12:1, NKJV). The body participates in worship. If worship involves the body—kneeling, lifting hands, dancing, singing—then sexual intimacy, the deepest bodily union in covenant, is theological by nature. When spiritual maturity meets sexual maturity, marriage becomes holistic. The soul does not outrun the body, and the body does not outrun the soul. This is the restoration of Eden—not the innocence before the Fall, but the *integration after the Cross*.

Language is one of God's first gifts to humanity. God creates by speaking. Adam exercises dominion by naming. Jesus heals by naming. Naming restores agency. When couples lack language for desire, they cannot narrate their sexual story. Silence narrates for them. Silence breeds confusion.

Confusion breeds distance. Distance breeds resentment. Redeeming formation requires naming: naming fear. Naming desire. Naming wounds. Naming hopes. Naming preferences. Naming embarrassment. These names are not indulgent; they are *incarnational*. Once named, narratives must be reframed. A husband who believed his desire was dangerous must reframe desire as *devotion*. A wife who believed her pleasure was shameful must reframe pleasure as *participation*. A believer who believes sex is merely functional must reframe sex as *covenant communion*.

Reframing shifts the narrative from survival to delight. Without reframing, novelty becomes a distraction rather than intimacy. Without reframing, technique becomes performance rather than communion. Redemption requires understanding not just what to do with the body, but what God intended for the body.

At this point in their journey, many couples feel both exposed and relieved. *Exposed*, because they can finally name why sex has been difficult. *Relieved*, because difficulty is no longer interpreted as failure. This relief is not trivial; it is sacred. Relief is the ground on which delight is built. Delight does not emerge in the absence of difficulty. Delight emerges when difficulty is met with *safety* instead of shame. When lovers stop bracing and begin breathing, the nervous system opens to pleasure. When lovers stop apologizing for desire and begin receiving it, the soul opens to intimacy. Pleasure is not shallow. Pleasure is theological. Psalm 36 declares, *"You give them drink from Your river of delights"* (v. 8, NIV). Delight is part of the inheritance of the righteous. God is not threatened by pleasure; He is the author of it. If sin is the distortion of delight, then redemption is the restoration of it. Marriage is the covenant workshop where this restoration unfolds in the body.

A SucSEXful marriage does not stop at healing; it proceeds to *enjoyment*. A healed garden is meant to bear fruit. What shame concealed, delight reveals. What fear suppressed, desire awakens. What silence muted, intimacy gives voice. Pleasure becomes testimony: *We belong to each other without fear.*

When couples discover that sexuality in covenant is not a compromise with the flesh but a celebration of design, their imagination changes, they stop striving for compatibility and begin cultivating curiosity. They stop performing and begin participating.

They stop treating sex as a duty and begin treating it as communion. Formation prepared the soil; now the garden is ready for cultivation.

Formation explains how we learned to hide; redemption teaches us how to come out of hiding. Marriage becomes the workshop where shame is confronted, not by condemnation, but by *communion*. The gospel does not merely save the soul; it restores the lover.

The cross not only reconciles us to God; it reopens the possibility of being fully known by another without fear of abandonment.

From a psychological perspective, healing in the sexual domain requires *safety*. The nervous system cannot enter arousal from a defensive posture. The body cannot receive pleasure while preparing for rejection. The brain cannot explore erotic curiosity while scanning for danger. For many couples, the first miracle in the bedroom is not orgasm; it is safety. For others, the first miracle is permission: permission to desire. Permission to pursue. Permission to receive. Permission to ask questions without fear of judgment. Permission to be awkward while learning new forms of intimacy. Permission to bless the body rather than critique it. Permission to delight rather than endure. Many believers have permission for sexual duty but not permission for *covenantal pleasure*.

Redemption reframes sex not as something to *"perform"* but as something to *"practice."* Performance demands flawless execution. Practice allows curiosity, failure, repetition, laughter, and growth. Performance produces anxiety. Practice produces skill and confidence. God did not command Adam and Eve to perform intimacy; He invited them to practice communion.

From a prophetic standpoint, the Church must reclaim sexual discipleship. We disciple believers in prayer, stewardship, worship, and evangelism, but we leave them to improvise sexual desire without guidance. Silence is not neutrality; silence is abdication. When the Church refuses to speak about the body, pornography becomes the primary discipler. When pastors refuse to speak about desire, fear becomes the primary interpreter. When marriages refuse to speak about pleasure, resentment becomes the primary witness.

From a pastoral standpoint, redemption requires curiosity without accusation. Curiosity says, *"Help me understand you."* The accusation says, *"Prove yourself to me."* Curiosity opens the door to intimacy. Accusation shuts it. In a covenant, curiosity becomes an act of pursuit. Many couples discover that their marriage did not fail due to a lack of love but due to a lack of curiosity.

From a clinical standpoint, healing in sexual intimacy often requires the nervous system to learn new patterns.

Avoidant partners must learn to stay present without fleeing emotionally. Anxious partners must learn to trust without clinging. Traumatized partners must learn embodiment without dissociating. Shame-formed partners must learn to receive without apology. These are not merely spiritual tasks; they are neurophysiological ones.

Redemption does not erase the past; it reinterprets it. The gospel does not ask, *"Did you come to marriage with perfect sexual formation?"* but *"Will you allow covenant to heal what formation distorted?"* The question is not whether desire was malformed, but whether desire can be *disciplined.* Pleasure can be sanctified. Curiosity can be holy. Arousal can be covenantal. The body can be blessed.

This reframing allows couples to move from avoiding sexual sin to pursuing sexual communion. Communion requires presence. Presence requires vulnerability. Vulnerability requires safety. Safety requires covenant. Covenant requires pursuit. Pursuit requires courage. Courage requires healing. Healing requires honesty. Honesty requires language. Language requires discipleship. And discipleship requires the Church to stop whispering about what God never blushed to create.

If the enemy cannot destroy the covenant, he will drain it of delight. If he cannot seduce the marriage bed into unfaithfulness, he will starve it into indifference. If he cannot corrupt intimacy through impurity, he will suffocate it through silence. But intimacy is returning to many marriages, not through novelty alone, but through *redemption*. Delight is returning. Curiosity is returning. Play is returning. Pleasure is returning. Safety is returning. Tenderness is returning. And with them returns a theology of embodiment that the Church nearly forgot: that holiness and pleasure are not enemies, that covenant is not the death of desire, and that erotic union is not merely permissible, it is *blessed.*

You were not formed only for restraint; you were formed for delight. The gospel does not merely rescue sinners; it restores lovers. Desire was never meant to be feared; it was meant to be given. Pleasure was never meant to be hidden; it was meant to be received. Covenant was never meant to be endured; it was meant to be *enjoyed.* Formation has prepared the soil. The garden awaits.

Covenant was never meant to be endured. It was meant to be enjoyed. Formation prepared the soil. The garden awaits.

Reflection Questions

1. In what ways was your sexual formation shaped more by silence than by discipleship?
2. What emotions (fear, anxiety, excitement, shame, curiosity) arise when you think about sexual intimacy?
3. How has your understanding of God shaped the way you relate to your own body?
4. What conversations about intimacy have you avoided in your marriage, and why?
5. Where do you need to extend curiosity toward your spouse rather than assumption or accusation?

Application Practice — Curiosity & Safety Week

For the next seven days, practice asking your spouse one question about intimacy without pressure, without defensiveness, and without an agenda. Use language like:

- "Help me understand…"
- "When you said ____, what did you feel?"
- "How does your body respond when…?"

- "What do you wish I knew about…?"
- "What helps you feel safe with me?"

Curiosity is a pursuit. Pursuit is covenantal. Covenant creates safety. Safety enables communion.

Prayer

Lord, You are the God who formed our bodies, our desires, and our capacity for intimacy. You did not design us for hiding but for communion. Where fear has silenced us, give us courage. Where shame has wounded us, give us healing. Where disappointment has hardened us, give us tenderness. Teach us to bless one another not with mere duty but with delight.

Redeem our formation, restore our curiosity, and make our marriage a place where safety and intimacy grow together. In Jesus' name, amen.

Blessing to the Wife

I bless you, my wife. I bless your heart, your body, and your belongings. I bless your femininity as a gift and not a burden, as beauty and not a liability. I bless your desire as holy, your voice as needed, and your presence as treasure.

I honor the story you lived before me, and I receive the story you are living with me. Where fear has silenced you, may safety give you speech. Where shame has wounded you, may tenderness give you healing. You are bone of my bone and flesh of my flesh. I bless you with peace, dignity, and joy in our union. You are not alone in this covenant.

Blessing to the Husband

I bless you, my husband. I bless your strength, your tenderness, and your capacity to pursue. I bless your masculinity as dignity and not performance. I bless your desire as a gift and not pressure. I honor your story, the victories you celebrate and the wounds you seldom name. Where expectations have burdened you, may grace give you rest. Where silence has isolated you, may connection give you courage. You are bone of my bone and flesh of my flesh. I bless you with confidence, honor, and joy in our union. You are not alone in this covenant.

Affirmation

Our bodies are not battlegrounds — they are temples. Our desire is not shameful — it is formed for communion. Our marriage is not merely permitted — it is blessed.

***

The Role of Redemption in Sexual Intimacy. Healing prepares the body for desire, and desire prepares the marriage for communion. When shame is quieted, and fear loses its grip, intimacy no longer feels dangerous; it feels sacred. Safety is the beginning of restoration; delight is its natural fruit.

***

Chapter 8

SucSEXful Marriage: From Prohibition to Passion

***

"Eat, friends, drink, and drink your fill of love." — Song of Songs 5:1, NIV

"The body is not an obstacle to spirituality; it is the theater of redemption." — Hans Urs von Balthasar.

Desire does not begin in the bedroom. It begins in the imagination when it feels invited, in the body when it feels safe, and in the soul when it feels welcomed. Before lovers touch, hearts must open. Before clothing is removed, fear must be dismissed.

Scripture does not treat erotic delight as a concession to marriage but as a celebration of covenant: *"Kiss me, full on the mouth!"* (Song 1:2, MSG). Scripture does not apologize for sexual longing. It blesses it. Desire is older than shame. Pleasure is older than sin. Delight is older than guilt.

In Eden, desire was not temptation but design. God did not build a lecture hall. He planted a garden. Gardens are sensual spaces, full of taste, texture, color, fragrance, and encounter. Before the Fall, bodies were not hidden. Nakedness was not vulnerability; it was communion. Pleasure was not suspect; it was blessed.

Marriage is the covenant restoration of Edenic intimacy, not in innocence but in redemption. Delight returns not through naivety but through healing. Covenant makes lovers safe enough to pursue without fear of abandonment, to reveal without fear of ridicule, and to receive without fear of rejection. The marriage bed is not the site of shame's triumph; it is the site of shame's undoing.

Sexual delight in Scripture is not an accident of biology but a feature of design. The woman invites, *"Let him kiss me with the kisses of his mouth!"* (Song 1:2, NIV). The man admires, *"You are altogether beautiful, my darling; there is no flaw in you"* (Song 4:7, NIV). Mutual admiration is the language of Eden restored.

Rabbi Akiva once declared, "All the writings are holy, but the Song of Songs is the holy of holies." He did not elevate it because it was chaste, but because it was embodied. Israel did not blush at the body. Israel blessed the body. Gregory of Nyssa echoed this, writing that bodily union within marriage "becomes a path to the invisible."

Marriage is not a tolerated territory for sexuality. It is consecrated territory for it.

Paul deepens this language: *"Your bodies are temples of the Holy Spirit"* (1 Corinthians 6:19, NIV). Temples are not hidden from God. They are where God meets His people. If the body is a temple, then marital union becomes embodied worship, not in performance but in joyful, sacrificial giving and receiving. Theology without embodiment becomes abstraction. Embodiment without theology becomes instinct. Covenant holds them together.

Communion offers another lens. Communion is giving and receiving. It nourishes. It unites. It seals a covenant in the material world. Marital union shares this character. When lovers give and receive pleasure, they do not merely climax. They commune. The body becomes the liturgy of love.

Erotic Literacy and Embodied Design

In Scripture, *delight* is not opposed to holiness; delight is part of holiness. When delight disappears, so does a dimension of worship. A *SucSEXful* marriage restores Edenic delight, temple embodiment, and communion union. It allows lovers to say not merely, "We did not sin," but *"We enjoyed, we delighted, we belonged, and God was not absent." Song of Songs* refuses to separate pleasure from holiness. It refuses to divide embodiment from spirituality. It refuses to treat desire as secular and covenant as sacred. Instead, it merges them until they are indistinguishable. The lovers taste, smell, touch, admire, pursue, and enjoy. Their words arouse. Their words bless. Their words awaken. Erotic joy is not peripheral to the text; it is central. To have a *SucSEXful* marriage is to reclaim desire as covenantal rather than carnal. When the Church lost the language of delight, the marriage bed began to starve. Redemption restores that language, not for indulgence but for communion. God does not merely tolerate sexual intimacy within marriage; He attends it.

Lovers are not mind-readers; they are translators of desire. Erotic communication begins long before penetration. It begins with how a husband notices his wife without demanding her, how a wife acknowledges her husband's desire without shaming him, and how spouses allow themselves to be seen without apology. Language prepares the nervous system for pleasure by reducing ambiguity and increasing safety. Ambiguity is the enemy of anticipation. When lovers communicate with clarity, the body relaxes into receptivity. Many Christians assume sex should come *naturally,* but instinct rarely substitutes for knowledge. Lovers must learn from one another. They must learn rhythms, sensitivities, pacing, pressure, and preferences. *Song of Songs* models this with startling tenderness: *"You've captured my heart with one glance of your eyes"*

(Song 4:9, NIV). Lovers pay attention. They name what they notice. They offer feedback with curiosity rather than critique. Feedback is not complaint; it is choreography. Without it, desire becomes guesswork.

Erotic play also matters. Play dismantles pressure, and pressure suffocates pleasure. Couples who can laugh during intimacy often climax more easily because laughter signals safety. Safety signals surrender. Surrender is a prerequisite for orgasm. Pornography reduces sex to technique. Covenant expands it to a relationship. Pornography teaches performance. Covenant teaches participation.

Many believers arrive at marriage with profound spiritual formation and profound sexual illiteracy. They know how to pray but not how to climax. They know how to fast but not how to receive pleasure without guilt. They know how to serve God faithfully, but not how to pursue their spouse erotically. Sexual literacy is not vulgar or secular; it is dignified stewardship of covenant bodies. Arousal does not begin in the genitals; it begins in the imagination. Before the body responds, the mind must feel invited, and before the mind awakens, the soul must feel safe. Safety is not the opposite of passion; safety is the precondition of passion. Passion without safety is adrenaline. Passion with safety is surrender. Erotic desire does not behave the same way for all bodies.

Many men experience what researchers call *spontaneous desire:* arousal arrives quickly, often visually, and with minimal warm-up. Many women experience what is called *responsive desire:* arousal awakens through connection, context, anticipation, and pacing. Neither pattern is superior; neither is dysfunction. There are two ways the body says *yes.*

Orgasm also follows distinct patterns. For most men, orgasm follows a predictable sequence: arousal, erection, stimulation, climax, ejaculation, and refractory reset. For women, orgasm is typically clitoral in origin, not vaginal. Penetration can support climax but rarely replaces clitoral stimulation. This is not a failure of intercourse; it is the design of creation. The clitoris contains approximately 8,000 nerve endings, more than double that of the penis, and its sole purpose is pleasure. God did not hide this; He highlighted it.

Breath, rhythm, and pelvic floor engagement significantly influence climax. The pelvic floor is not merely anatomical support; it is erotic infrastructure. Gentle contraction increases sensitivity, and relaxation increases receptivity. During arousal, blood flow increases, breath deepens, and the nervous system shifts from vigilance to surrender.

Climax is not merely tension but release. Hormones accompany this process like liturgical elements. Testosterone fuels desire.

Estrogen increases sensitivity and lubrication. Dopamine reinforces pleasure and pursuit. Serotonin stabilizes mood and satisfaction. Oxytocin binds lovers through post-orgasmic attachment. These are not evolutionary leftovers; they are divine choreography.

Novelty also shapes erotic responsiveness. The nervous system enjoys variation, not to chase endless new partners, as pornography offers, but to experience the same beloved in new ways. Novelty does not require transgression; it requires curiosity. Variation in position, setting, pacing, sensory focus, or sequence can awaken desire without compromising holiness. When lovers encounter each other with anticipation rather than obligation, the marriage bed becomes a vineyard rather than a chore. Pornography counterfeits novelty by offering novelty without belonging. Covenant offers belonging with novelty. One offers climax without communion. The other offers communion that enhances the climax. Pornography teaches performance; covenant teaches participation. Pornography teaches consumption; covenant teaches delight. Pornography teaches comparison; covenant teaches curiosity.

A *SucSEXful* marriage learns the body of the beloved not as a problem to solve but as a garden to cultivate.

Lovers become students. They discover the geography of arousal, the landscapes of pleasure, and the seasons of desire. They do not rush to climax; they explore pleasure. They do not demand orgasm; they invite it. The goal is not efficiency but communion. In communion, climax becomes more than release; it becomes revelation.

For clarity and dignity, and without vulgarity, we name the relevant anatomy as God designed it:

- *Penis* — the primary male sexual organ for penetration and ejaculation.
- *Testes* — produce sperm and testosterone; also sensitive to touch.
- *Vulva* — external female genitalia, including labia and clitoral structures.
- *Clitoris* — primary female pleasure organ with 8,000+ nerve endings; central to female orgasm.
- *G-Spot Region* — internal pleasure area along the anterior vaginal wall; pleasure varies among women.

- *Vagina* — internal canal for penetration, birth, and menstrual flow; highly elastic and responsive.
- *Breasts* — sexual and nurturing organs with hormonal and erotic sensitivity.
- *Pelvic Floor* — the muscular system is crucial for arousal, orgasm, and sexual health.

None of these body parts is profane. They are not impurities to be endured or embarrassments to be hidden. God made them. He built them with sensitivity, responsiveness, lubrication capacity, erection capability, elasticity, and pleasure potential. Sexual literacy honors design rather than erasing shame with silence.

Orgasm is also part of this literacy. For most men, orgasm follows arousal predictably. For many women, arousal is contextual, dynamic, and may peak in waves rather than a single ascent. Female climax is often clitoral rather than vaginal. Penetration can enhance but rarely replaces clitoral stimulation. This is not dysfunction; it is design. When couples misunderstand design, they misinterpret differences as deficiencies.

Orgasm also bonds. God embedded the body with biochemical pathways that reinforce attachment:

- *Oxytocin* increases trust and bonding.
- *Dopamine* reinforces pleasure and pursuit.
- *Serotonin* stabilizes mood and reduces anxiety.
- *Testosterone* fuels desire and drive.
- *Estrogen* increases sensitivity and arousal.

These are not evolutionary accidents; they are signatures of intent. Vaginal lubrication signals readiness. Semen carries seeds. Orgasm carries bonding. Fluids are sacramental symbols of covenant embodiment. Sex is not sterile; it is generative, emotionally, spiritually, and physiologically. When believers grasp this, they stop treating their bodies as secular machines and begin treating them as sacred instruments of union.

Playfulness plays a vital role in erotic intimacy. Many Christian couples assume maturity requires seriousness, but seriousness is not the engine of desire; play is. In *Song of Songs*, the lovers tease, invite, praise, imagine, and enjoy. Their delight is not solemn. It is sensory and exploratory.

This is not immaturity; this is Eden restored. Play is not the opposite of holiness; play is the opposite of fear. Fear constricts the body; play opens it. Fear demands performance; play allows discovery. Lovers who can laugh together during intimacy often climax more easily because laughter tells the nervous system it is safe to surrender.

Novelty also supports erotic vitality. The nervous system enjoys variation, not to chase endless new partners, but to experience the same beloved in new ways. Pornography trades in novelty without belonging. Covenant offers belonging without betrayal, where novelty emerges through curiosity rather than comparison. Novelty may include new rhythms, new pacing, new order of operations, new sensory focus, or simply more intentional slowness. None of this requires transgression. Sacred exploration does not imitate pornography; it redeems discovery.

Covenant also protects erotic vulnerability. Modern culture treats sex as entertainment. The Church has sometimes treated sex as a danger. Covenant treats sex as communion. Communion does not trivialize intimacy nor fear it; it honors intimacy by assigning to it meaning. Without a covenant, vulnerability is risky. With covenant, vulnerability becomes welcome. Exclusive belonging makes lovers safe enough to reveal themselves.

Fidelity is not merely moral; fidelity is erotic. To be chosen without fear of replacement awakens security. Security awakens surrender. Surrender awakens pleasure. Pleasure awakens worship. Covenant is not the death of desire; it is the sanctuary of desire. Sex is rarely just about sex. It is about attachment, safety, memory, expectation, and meaning. Many marital conflicts around intimacy are not conflicts of morality or desire but conflicts of the nervous system and attachment. Bodies remember what minds rationalize and what theology redeems only slowly.

From an attachment perspective, the "bedroom" is where the nervous system reveals its loyalties. The anxiously attached spouse often fears abandonment and may pursue sex for reassurance. Desire becomes a liturgy of closeness: *"Hold me so I know you will not leave."* The avoidantly attached spouse may fear engulfment and withdraw from intimacy to protect autonomy. Desire becomes a threat of intrusion: *"If I let you close, I will lose myself."* Neither pattern is rebellion; both are protection strategies learned long before marriage. Trauma complicates this further. Trauma does not need to be violent to be formative. It can be ridicule, coercion, betrayal, premature exposure, religious shaming, comparison, or chronic rejection. Trauma teaches the nervous system that the body is not a safe place to feel. During intimacy, trauma survivors may dissociate, go numb, tense involuntarily, freeze, or shut down.

These are not moral failures; they are survival reflexes. The body protects itself when it does not trust that pleasure will be safe.

Healing in this territory is gentle and slow. The nervous system must learn safety before it can experience surrender. Surrender is the doorway to pleasure. Without safety, there is obligation, performance, or endurance, but not delight. Covenant offers the ideal environment for this re-learning because covenant promises presence. Presence calms the nervous system. Presence invites breath. Breath invites embodiment. Embodiment invites pleasure.

Consent also takes on a distinct shape in a covenant. Modern culture treats consent primarily as legal permission to access the body. Covenant treats consent as joyful participation of the beloved. Consent in covenant is not merely *"You may"* but *"I want to."* Two lovers give themselves, not just their bodies. When both offer willing participation, sex becomes communion rather than transaction. When trauma is present, consent becomes layered. There are micro-consents within intimacy: *"May I touch here?" "Is this pressure good?" "Do you want slower?" "Do you want more?"* These questions dismantle fear and build safety. Safety allows the nervous system to stop monitoring danger and begin experiencing sensation. Sensation opens the door to desire.

For many couples, the moment of breakthrough arrives not at climax but at presence. When a spouse with a wounded history remains fully in their body during intimacy without numbing, bracing, or leaving, resurrection has begun. The body learns that touch can be safe again. The heart learns that intimacy can be mutual. The spirit learns that delight is not forbidden.

In trauma-informed intimacy, healing precedes novelty. Novelty precedes play. Play precedes ecstasy. Ecstasy precedes worship. A *SucSEXful* marriage learns to move slowly enough for the nervous system to trust pleasure, and boldly enough for desire to awaken. What once felt frightening becomes curiosity. What once felt obligatory becomes a pursuit. What once felt sinful becomes sacramental.

Sex is often imagined as physical with spiritual consequences. Scripture imagines it as spiritual with physical expression. *"The two shall become one flesh"* (Ephesians 5:31, NKJV) is not a metaphor alone; it is a mystery. The early Church fathers described marital union as both symbolic and sacramental, symbolic of Christ and the Church, and sacramental as a means of embodied grace between spouses. Erotic intimacy unfolds within three theological movements:

- *The Garden* — where nakedness and delight coexist without shame.
- *The Temple* — where the body becomes the meeting place of covenant.
- *Communion* — where lovers give and receive in union.

Gardens are sensory, temples are sacred, and communion is participatory. Sex in marriage draws from all three. This is why avoidance can become spiritual warfare: if the enemy cannot destroy the covenant through infidelity, he will often drain it through indifference. Distance kills intimacy long before adultery does. When spouses persist in union, their bodies preach what their mouths have not yet articulated: *we are still one.*

Many couples arrive at this point in their formation relieved. Relief is sacred. Relief signals that pleasure is no longer interpreted as rebellion but as a blessing. Pleasure is not shallow; it is theological. Psalm 36 declares, *"You give them drink from Your river of delights"* (v. 8, NIV). Delight is part of the inheritance of the righteous. God is not threatened by pleasure; He authored it. If sin distorts pleasure, redemption restores it.

A *SucSEXful* marriage does not stop at healing; it proceeds to enjoyment. A healed garden is meant to bear fruit.

When couples discover that sexuality in covenant is not a concession to the flesh but a celebration of design, their imagination changes, they stop striving for compatibility and begin cultivating curiosity. They stop treating sex as a duty and begin treating it as a delight. Formation prepared the soil. Now the garden invites cultivation.

Many couples long for intimacy that is both passionate and spiritual, but they have been discipled into a divided world where the body worships in one direction, and the spirit worships in another. In Scripture, these two were never meant to be separated. Covenant joins flesh and spirit into one. Erotic communion is not a departure from holiness; it is an expression of it. The God who became flesh in Christ does not blush at embodied love. He blesses it. Blessing the body is not a sentimental gesture; it is a theological act. Many believers bless meals, homes, and children, but have never blessed their spouse's body. Yet Adam's first recorded words in Scripture were not a sermon, but a blessing spoken over Eve's body: *"This is now bone of my bones and flesh of my flesh"* (Genesis 2:23, NKJV). Before Adam preached, he admired. Before he named sin, he named beauty. Covenant begins with a blessing.

Communion offers a deep parallel. Communion is a liturgy of giving and receiving. It nourishes, unites, and seals a covenant through the body. Sex in marriage shares this liturgical pattern.

Lovers give themselves fully without fear of abandonment. They receive one another without fear of comparison. Their bodies become sacraments of belonging. They taste and see that the covenant is good. Post-coital bonding is part of this communion. After climax, oxytocin surges, and the nervous system enters a state of rest and openness. This is not laziness; this is bonding. To roll away immediately or to hide the body is to interrupt communion. To linger, breathe, touch, and hold is to seal it. Many marital arguments could be healed not through confrontation but through communion, through bodies that belong to one another without fear.

In a *SucSEXful* marriage, spiritual maturity enhances erotic delight rather than suppressing it. Lovers pursue holiness not by restraining desire but by sanctifying it. They learn that desire is not the enemy of worship; desire is one of the ways the body worships. They do not have sex to relieve tension; they have sex to reveal love. They do not climax to escape the world; they climax to commune with the one to whom they belong. This is the restoration of Eden: delight without shame, desire without fear, and union without hiding.

If the enemy cannot destroy the covenant, he will drain it of delight. If he cannot seduce lovers into infidelity, he will starve them into apathy. If he cannot corrupt intimacy through impurity, he will suffocate it through silence.

But dignity is returning to the marriage bed. Curiosity is returning. Play is returning. Pleasure is returning. Safety is returning. And with them returns a theology of embodiment that the Church nearly forgot: that holiness and pleasure are companions, not adversaries. Covenant is not the funeral of desire; it is its flourishing. Erotic union is not merely permitted; it is blessed. You were not formed only for restraint; you were formed for delight. The gospel does not merely rescue sinners; it restores lovers. Desire was never meant to be feared; it was meant to be given. Pleasure was never meant to be hidden; it was meant to be received. Covenant was never meant to be endured; it was meant to be enjoyed.

The garden is open. The vineyard awaits.

Reflection

Reflection converts desire from instinct into awareness. Begin with yourself:

1. What delights me that I have never named?
2. What pleasures have I withheld from myself out of guilt or fear?
3. What expectations did I bring into intimacy that I never examined?

4. What stories about sex did I inherit from family, culture, or church without question?

5. Where does my body still brace rather than rest?

Then consider your spouse:

- What relaxes them?
- What reassures them?
- What pressures them?
- What delights them?
- Where do they open?
- Where do they withdraw?
- What has never been spoken aloud between us?

Then consider your union:

- Where does our intimacy feel alive?
- Where does it feel silent?
- Where does it feel predictable?

- Where does it feel unpracticed?
- Where does it feel sacred?

Finally, consider God:

- Where have I assumed God was absent from my pleasure?
- Where have I imagined holiness as the opposite of desire?
- How is the Spirit inviting us toward delight rather than merely tolerance?

Reflection prepares the imagination for communion.

Application

Application is not performance; it is participation. Choose a time when both spouses are unhurried, emotionally present, and physically relaxed. Share one desire, one fear, and one curiosity—without fixing or defending.

- Desire says: "I would love…"
- Fear says: "I worry…"
- Curiosity says: "I wonder…"

Do not aim for intercourse. Do not aim for orgasm. Do not aim for resolution. Aim for disclosure. *Honesty* reopens the garden.

For the next week, treat intimacy as vineyard cultivation. Explore slowly. Honor feedback. Let laughter be welcome. Let awkwardness be acceptable. Let pleasure be unhurried. Lovers are not born; they are learned.

Prayer

Father, thank You for designing our bodies with sensitivity, our marriages with covenant, and our desire with purpose. Where shame has silenced us, give us language. Where fear has tightened us, give us rest. Where trauma has guarded us, give us safety. Where silence has separated us, give us communion.

Teach us to pursue one another with tenderness, to receive one another with joy, and to reveal ourselves without fear. Make our marriage bed a sanctuary of play, curiosity, and delight. Restore to us the garden we lost through hiding and awaken in us the confidence of lovers who belong to one another without comparison or condemnation.

Let pleasure be holy. Let touch be healing. Let surrender be safe. Let our bodies worship You through delight. In Jesus' name, amen.

Affirmation

Our covenant is blessed. Our bodies are temples. Our pleasure is holy. We cultivate intimacy with joy, curiosity, and delight.

***

When intimacy is understood as sacred and mutual, it can become one of marriage's greatest joys. But even healthy passion can fade under pressure, misunderstanding, fatigue, or unspoken wounds. What begins as delight can quietly turn into distance if it is not tended carefully.

***

Chapter 9

SOS: Save Our Sex

***

Sex doesn't collapse in a marriage with one dramatic moment. It slips away quietly. It goes missing between late-night emails, school drop-offs, church calendars, and "maybe tomorrow." It fades between two phones in the dark. It hides behind courtesy and fatigue. There's no fight, no slammed door, no epic betrayal, just two people who used to reach for each other and now reach for their chargers. They lie side by side, scrolling. Notifications flicker across their faces. A small laugh, a sigh, a turned shoulder. Then darkness. Nothing happened. That's what hurt. Not rejection, not argument, *absence*. The kind of absence you can't explain without sounding dramatic. The kind of absence that doesn't make headlines but still hollows out the heart a little at a time.

The Quiet Erosion of Intimacy

Sex doesn't have to vanish to be missed. It only has to feel complicated. It only has to feel like one more thing you have to initiate, *schedule*, or negotiate. Many husbands and wives are not aching for orgasm; they are aching to be wanted, to be pursued, to be wondered about. They miss being looked at with hunger, not just familiarity. They miss being someone's delight, not just someone's responsibility. Most sexless marriages are not full of resentment; they are full of *resignation*. There's love, there's loyalty, there's partnership, and there's even prayer. But there's no spark. No playful pull. No curiosity.

No flirtation that builds into something more. The marriage becomes faithful but famished. It's hard to confess this to anyone, especially in church, because desire sounds like carnality and longing sounds like weakness. And so, couples press on with polite silence, convincing themselves that maturity means learning how to live without touch, without pursuit, without delight.

Meanwhile, the Scriptures have no such shyness. *Song of Songs* brims with hunger, metaphor, scent, skin, invitation, poetry, and atmosphere. Eden does not blush. Heaven does not apologize for longing.

The modern marriage bed, however, often carries a different liturgy, one of exhaustion and self-consciousness. Parents collapse into it. Volunteers fall asleep in it. Ministers study in it. Phones dominate it. Bills sit on the nightstand beside it. The bed becomes an office, a planning centre, a prayer bench, a co-sleeping station, a charging dock; anything except what it was in Genesis: *"one flesh."*

Desire Hides, Not Dies

Desire does not usually die in marriage; it hides. It hides behind laundry piles and ministry calendars. It hides behind body shame and comparison. It hides behind years of pregnancy and postpartum recovery. It hides behind good intentions and bad communication. It hides behind the kind of fear nobody names: the fear of wanting more than you're getting and the shame of admitting you want it at all.

Ask any couple who has gone quiet in bed, and they will tell you: it's not that they don't care, it's that they don't know how to bridge the distance anymore. Initiation feels loaded. Rejection feels humiliating. Silence feels safer than asking. And the longer the silence is chosen, the harder it becomes to reveal desire without feeling needy or dramatic.

There is no clinical term for lying inches from someone you love and feeling untouchable. No statistic measures how lonely it feels to go to bed with the same person every night and feel gently ignored. Therapists define a sexless marriage as having fewer than ten sexual encounters a year, but couples feel the famine long before they reach that number. Bodies keep count long before calendars do.

Andre and Keisha eventually learned that their stalemate wasn't indifference; it was self-protection.

Keisha feared rejection, so she waited to be invited. Andre feared humiliation, so he stopped inviting. Neither of them lacked desire; they lacked safety. And without safety, the body keeps its distance, even under the covers.

Spiritual and Sexual Disconnect

Christians sometimes over-spiritualize this problem. They assume desire is a luxury, not a language. But Scripture never treats sex as an optional upgrade or a marital bonus feature. It treats it as covenantal communion, an embodied "yes" to union. In Genesis, before there was ministry, or mission, or children, or community, there was nakedness without shame. Before purpose, there was pleasure. Before co-labouring, there was delight. Before tasks, there was touch. So, when sex goes missing from marriage, something weighty is lost, not because sex is everything, but because sex carries things that nothing else can carry: pursuit, playfulness, vulnerability, urgency, union, and that mysterious feeling of being chosen again.

It is not merely a physical act; it is a renewal ceremony disguised as desire.

When sex becomes rare, spouses don't stop loving each other; they stop knowing how to reach for each other. Desire becomes awkward. Touch feels risky.

Pursuit feels childish. Humor feels inappropriate. The marriage becomes polite. Functional. Cooperative. Respectful even. But tenderness evaporates. And once tenderness goes, delight goes with it.

The Hidden Struggles in Marriage

It would be easier if the cause were straightforward. If someone had betrayed someone. If there were pornography, infidelity, or secret fantasies involved. At least then the wound would have a name. But many sexless marriages are not wounded by scandal; they are wounded by life.

Fatigue is a thief. Ministry is a thief. Children are beautiful thieves. Travel is a thief. Chronic stress steals curiosity: anxiety steals spontaneity; shame steals pursuit. Nobody warns you about this in premarital counselling. Everyone talks about communication and finances. Few mention how difficult it becomes to stay adorable for each other when you're both exhausted. This hunger sits quietly in church. It sits quietly in small groups. It sits quietly in Christian counselling offices where wives whisper that they miss being held, and husbands whisper that they miss being wanted.

And both leave with the suspicion that admitting this somehow makes them less spiritual. As if holiness were measured by how little pleasure we need.

As if desire were something you grow out of, like teenage impulsiveness. But Scripture never treats desire as childish. *The entire Song of Songs* is a book-length celebration of erotic pursuit, longing, fragrance, skin, lips, breasts, spice, gardens, delight, and mutual invitation. It is the only book of the Bible that does not apologize for passion. It does not make intimacy clinical, comedic, or crude. It makes it sacred.

The Importance of Desire in Marriage

If sexlessness were only about lust or orgasm, we could dismiss it as a preference. But it is about belonging. It is about being chosen again. It is about hearing with the body what the vows promised with the mouth. It is about recognizing your spouse not just as a partner or parent or co-laborer, but as a mystery. The peculiar pain of a sexless marriage is that the hunger has no language. If you say nothing, you suffer. If you say something, you risk sounding dramatic or needy. If you initiate and get turned down, the rejection echoes. If you stop initiating, the silence deepens. Eventually, both spouses start interpreting stillness as disinterest, even if both are waiting for the other to make the first move.

The truth is, it is easier to go without touch than it is to confess desire. It is easier to feel unwanted than it is to risk humiliation. Many marriages find themselves in a stalemate neither person chose, but both participate in.

Sex becomes like prayer: everyone agrees it matters; many wish it happened more, and few know how to begin again after a long drought.

Reigniting Desire

Desire is resilient, but it needs invitation. It needs playfulness. It needs surprise. It needs an atmosphere that isn't saturated with responsibility. It needs to live somewhere other than under fluorescent lights and unending to-do lists. It needs a place to breathe. Christian couples sometimes assume the only solution is more discipline: schedule sex, set reminders, optimize calendars, be intentional. And yes, rhythm helps.

But sex is not a task; it is a language. It withers when reduced to duty. Duty may achieve frequency, but it cannot generate delight.

Delight requires discovery. Delight requires permission. Delight requires space to laugh and blush and experiment and ask.

The Role of Covenant in Intimacy

If marriage were a garden, then sex would not be the garden itself; it would be the water. The garden can survive a few days without watering, but after a drought, the soil becomes hard, and seeds that once sprouted easily now take more work. Hard soil is not rebellion; it is neglect. It is waiting for rain.

Many couples pray for rain without daring to pick up the watering can. They ask God to fix desire without making room for delight.

They ask for erotic renewal without tenderness, for pursuit without playfulness, for communion without curiosity. But a covenant does not just preserve marriage; it sustains pleasure if we steward it.

The Sacredness of Sex in Marriage

Sex is not just fun; it is formative. It forms affection. It forms memory. It forms relief. It forms joy. It forms forgiveness. It forms unity. It forms humility. It forms vulnerability. It forms a unique kind of laughter that cannot be replicated in any other part of marriage.

It is one of the places where spouses become adolescents again together: awkward, playful, curious, and wonderfully human.

When sex disappears, marriages often lose laughter. Not the polite kind, the belly kind.

The kind where someone can't stop giggling because the pillow just fell off the bed, or someone tried something new and it felt ridiculous at first. Sexlessness removes the absurdity that keeps marriage from becoming a business partnership. Without erotic play, marriage becomes a limited liability company. God did not create marriage to be a limited liability company. He created it to be a covenant of communion, delight, dominion, and fruitfulness. The bed is not peripheral to that; it is sacramental.

It is the one place in marriage where nakedness is not vulnerability but worship.

The good news is that desire is not fragile. It does not die easily. It retreats when it does not feel safe. It curls inward like a flower waiting for sunlight. And sunlight does not have to be dramatic. A simple compliment. A lingering touch. A curious question. A shared memory. A playful nudge. A moment of eye contact that lasts one second longer than necessary. These are not techniques; they are invitations. *Sex* is not the only way lovers become lovers again.

Often, erotic renewal begins far earlier, through the smaller, quieter bridges of affection. The marriage bed is downstream from the kitchen, the car, the hallway, the bathroom sink, the church parking lot, and the grocery store. Desire is not born in the bedroom; it is revealed there. Sometimes the most spiritual thing a couple can do for their marriage is not fast more, serve more, or volunteer more, but to flirt again. To let themselves remember that joy is not childish, that curiosity is not immature, that laughter in the bedroom is not irreverent. God does not blush at delight. Heaven is not embarrassed by longing. Pleasure is not the opposite of holiness.

Sexual repair is rarely grand. It begins with tenderness. It begins with safety. It begins with small risks that restore trust. For some couples, the risk is naming the hunger. For others, it is saying "not now" without withholding affection.

For still others, it is receiving pursuit without suspicion. Each marriage returns to the bed through its own doorway, but the door is never locked from the outside.

If the enemy cannot destroy Christian marriages through infidelity, he will gladly settle for sterilizing them through distance. He will turn spouses into ministry partners instead of lovers. He will let them attend the same church, raise the same children, share the same last name, and never once taste the delight God intended them to enjoy. Holiness without joy is not holiness; it is starvation dressed in piety.

The call to *Save Our Sex* is not a call to idolize sex; it is a call to rescue covenant from dryness. It is a call to rediscover that bodies are not an afterthought of creation but an expression of it.

That God did not make us ghosts trapped in flesh, but images shaped in flesh. Incarnation is not a theological idea; it is a divine endorsement of embodiment. To revive sexual intimacy in marriage is not to return to adolescence; it is to honor covenant. It is to recognize that the vows we made with words must sometimes be renewed with skin. That touch and hunger and pleasure belong to marriage, not because they are base but because they are holy. Desire does not return by force. It returns by permission. And the permission is not primarily physical; it is covenantal.

In a modern world that treats intimacy as performance and sex as recreational, the gospel treats the marriage bed as a sanctuary where two image-bearers renew the vows their tongues once made, not by repeating the liturgy, but by embodying it.

The Repair of Intimacy

Intimacy breaks down when either spouse feels alone. Sometimes loneliness begins in the heart long before it reaches the body.

A husband may feel unwanted months before he stops initiating. A wife may feel unseen for years before she stops responding. And because neither has been taught how to confess loneliness without shame, avoidance appears. Avoidance is loneliness wearing armor. The repair of intimacy requires courage, but not the kind we imagine. The courage is not in grand gestures, but in small disclosures. To say, *"I miss belonging to you,"* is far riskier than to say, *"We need to work on our intimacy."* One is clinical and safe; the other is vulnerable and holy. Intimacy is not primarily a technique. It is a form of knowing.

For many couples, the marriage bed needs to become a covenant classroom again, not a place for performance, but a place to relearn how to delight in one another without pretense. Repair does not begin with intercourse. It begins with curiosity.

Curiosity softens fear. Curiosity rehumanizes the spouse who has become familiar. Curiosity makes space for desire to breathe again. When spouses stop being students of one another, desire becomes nostalgic rather than present. The early years of marriage are often fueled by novelty and the thrill of discovery. Later years require intentionality and the recovery of play. Covenant does not make desire automatic; covenant makes desire safe to pursue again.

Intimacy requires safety for wives far more often than we admit. Not because women are fragile, but because female desire is deeply connected to context, security, affirmation, and emotional attunement. A wife's body listens to the tone of her husband's voice long before it responds to the touch of his hand. Husbands often assume rejection where there is simply overwhelm.

When a wife says, *"not tonight,"* she may be saying, *"I am exhausted, overstimulated, or carrying twelve invisible burdens."* Her *"no"* is not always about sex; sometimes it is about survival. At the same time, husbands require pursuit far more often than our theology has allowed us to recognize. Male desire is frequently simplified into drive or hunger when it carries a profound longing to be wanted. To feel chosen. To be delighted in. Rejection wounds a husband not merely at the level of appetite, but at the level of identity. When husbands stop initiating, it is often not because desire has died, but because humiliation has accumulated. Both forms of longing are sacred. Neither is superior. Neither is childish. Neither is shameful.

Small Gestures of Repair

Repair often begins before either spouse realizes repair has begun. It begins in the hallway when he brushes past her intentionally, not sexual, just present. It begins in the kitchen when she hands him a mug of coffee, and their fingers linger a second longer than the mug requires. It begins when he compliments her hair without expecting anything to follow.

It begins when she touches his arm in church and whispers, *"You looked good today."* Small gestures carry disproportionate meaning when intimacy has gone quiet. One couple told me, *"We didn't start with sex. We started by noticing each other again."* That is a holy sentence. Noticing is one of the first languages of desire. Noticing says, *"I have not grown numb to you."* Noticing breaks the spell of familiarity that turns lovers into logistical teammates. Sometimes the moment of return is even smaller. A wife catches her husband watching her in the bathroom mirror, not with critique, but with wonder.

A husband walking by the laundry room and seeing the curve of his wife's shoulder as she folds towels, suddenly remembers that she is not only the mother of his children, but the woman he once risked everything to pursue. Memory is a powerful aphrodisiac when it is sanctified rather than sentimental. Tenderness also returns in laughter. The kind of laughter that spills out in bed when something awkward happens, and instead of shutting down, both spouses let themselves be human. Delight requires room for absurdity. If intimacy is a garden, laughter is the rain.

Covenant and Delight in Intimacy

As intimacy returns, sex becomes an invitation rather than a negotiation. The body remembers faster than the mind.

The body knows the difference between duty and desire. The body can tell when it is being chosen rather than used. When intimacy is repaired, sex becomes the embodied form of covenantal delight.

There is a theological beauty to this. In Scripture, covenants are renewed with signs. Bread and cup. Stones of remembrance. Sacrifices on altars.

Marriage has its own sacrament, not transacted in the sanctuary, but in the bedroom. Intimacy is where spouses renew the vows the pastor presided over years earlier.

Not because the original vows were weak, but because renewal is a divine pattern. Creation renews. Israel renews. The Church renews. Marriage renews.

In the garden, Adam and Eve were naked and unashamed. Their nakedness was not merely a lack of clothing; it was the absence of fear in the presence of another. Shame entered the story when they covered themselves, not because nakedness became unholy, but because vulnerability became unsafe.

Redemption is the slow reversal of that instinct. In Christ, the covenant restores what fear stole. Intimacy becomes worship when the marriage bed becomes the place where nakedness and belonging coexist again.

When spouses delight in one another, they bear witness to the goodness of creation. The world treats sex as entertainment. The church too often treats it as a duty. Scripture treats it as delight. *"Drink deeply, O lovers,"* Song of Songs says. It is difficult to drink deeply when counting obligations or accumulating resentments. Delight requires surrender. Delight requires welcome. Delight requires saying, *"My body does not hesitate to belong to you,"* and hearing, *"Your body is not a burden to me."*

The Goal of Intimacy

As repair unfolds, the goal is not merely intercourse; it is communion.

Communion is when desire becomes mutual, when pursuit becomes reciprocal, when safety becomes assumed, and when delight becomes ordinary. Ordinary delight is better than cinematic passion. Cinematic passion fades. Ordinary delight is sustainable.

When sex returns to the marriage bed after a season of drought, it often does not return with cinematic perfection. It returns with humility. It returns with nervousness. It returns with gratitude.

The holiness of intimacy is not in its performance but in its honesty. Two image-bearers reaching for one another without fear, without pretense, without justification, that is the gospel embodied in covenant.

Reflection

Sometimes the most healing questions are the ones we have never asked ourselves out loud. Sit with these gently, without judgment:

1. When did intimacy begin to retreat in our marriage?
2. What was happening in our lives during that season?
3. Did I feel more abandoned or more overwhelmed?
4. Did my spouse feel more rejected or more invisible?
5. How do I feel when I am desired?
6. How do I feel when I am avoided?
7. How have I responded to the hunger of my own body?
8. How have I responded to the hunger of my spouse's body?
9. What is one curiosity I have never voiced?
10. What is one fear I have never admitted?

You are not answering these to fix anything today. You are learning to recognize your interior world so you can invite your spouse into it with dignity.

Activation — The Soft Start

For the next seven days, choose one form of invitation each day that does not pressure, perform, or demand. Let the body learn safety again.

Examples of invitations (not commands):

- Noticing
- Complimenting
- Touching without escalation
- Laughing together
- Confessing desire without panic
- Asking instead of assuming
- Pursuing without entitlement
- Receiving pursuit without suspicion

If intercourse happens, you do not need to congratulate yourselves. If it doesn't, you do not need to diagnose yourselves. You are rebuilding trust, not chasing frequency.

The goal is not sex. The goal is belonging, and sex grows out of belonging.

Prayer

Lord, You formed us from dust and breath, spirit and body. You called our bodies good. You called our union honorable. You blessed intimacy as delight, not duty. Restore tenderness where distance has settled. Restore curiosity where fear has lived. Restore belonging where silence has grown. Teach us to choose one another again, without panic, without pretense, without shame. Let intimacy return to our marriage, not as performance but as communion. Let our bodies speak the covenant our vows once declared. In Jesus' name, Amen.

Declaration (Spouse to Spouse)

I choose to desire you without demanding you. I choose to pursue you without pressuring you. Your body is not an obligation to me, and mine is not a bargaining chip to you. We belong to one another in affection, curiosity, and delight.

Affirmation (Personal)

- *Desire is not unspiritual.*
- *Delight is not unholy.*
- *Intimacy is not shameful.*
- *Sex in marriage is covenantal.*

***

Intimacy may begin with desire, but it is sustained by tenderness. Many marriages assume sex will keep them connected; more often, it is connection that keeps desire alive. If sex is the spark, touch is the oil that allows it to burn steadily rather than fade.

***

Chapter 10

The Power of Touch

***

She couldn't remember the last time he touched her without needing anything. Not to move her out of the way, not to pass her the car keys, not to get her attention, but just because her body was there, within reach. It wasn't that they didn't love each other. It wasn't that they were angry or distant or on the verge of collapse. They laughed. They planned. They parented. They worshipped. They solved problems together. But there was no warmth in the small spaces anymore. No hand across the lower back in the kitchen. No shoulder against shoulder on the couch. No hand-held prayers. No unhurried hugs. The marriage was intact, but the tenderness had leaked out.

Intimacy Loss Begins in the Small Spaces

Most marriages don't lose intimacy in the bedroom first. They lose it in the hallway. They lose it on the couch. They lose it in the car. They lose it in all the tiny, ordinary places where bodies once brushed past each other without flinching. Before a marriage becomes sexually quiet, it often becomes affectionally quiet.

And affection; simple, non-sexual, unhurried touch, is the oxygen of erotic intimacy.

Before Scripture introduces sex, it introduces touch. Before there were vows, children, or shared responsibilities, there were two bodies in a garden with no shame between them. They were naked and unashamed, not merely unclothed, but unguarded. Shame entered the story when touch became a risk instead of a gift. Covenant is God's answer to that risk. Covenant restores trust so affection can return without fear of rejection or humiliation.

The First Language of Intimacy

Most people think sexual desire is the first language of intimacy, but for many spouses, it is not. For many, the first language of intimacy is affection: the hand on the arm, the fingers in the hair, the head on the shoulder, the forehead kiss. These gestures do not lead to sex; they lead to safety. And safety is what desire needs to breathe.

Attachment science has been trying to teach us this for decades. Human bodies bond through touch long before they bond through words. Infants are soothed through skin-to-skin contact before they learn language. Adults are no different; we just disguise our need for comfort with competence. We call it stress.

We call it exhaustion. We call it being overwhelmed. But underneath those labels is often a very old need: to be held without having to earn it.

A Silent Longing for Touch

Andre didn't know how to explain that need without sounding childish. He was a grown man, a husband, a father, a provider. But when Keisha stopped touching him in the small ways, when she pulled her feet away on the couch, when she stopped kissing him in passing, when hugs became quick taps on the back, something inside him grew quiet. He didn't ask for more sex. He asked for contact. He asked for nearness. He asked to feel wanted without having to perform.

Keisha didn't withhold touch because she was indifferent. She withheld because her body was tired. Her days were full of small pulls on her attention; children's hands, ministry demands, notifications, and errands. By the end of the day, she had nothing left to offer. Her body was no longer a vehicle of invitation; it had become a vehicle of survival. Touch felt like one more demand. Their silence made sense. But the silence created distance. And then the distance created caution. And caution is where marriages begin to lose affection, not because love has died, but because bodies have forgotten how to relax in one another's presence.

Touch as Recognition and Comfort

Touch in marriage is not primarily sexual. It becomes sexual, but that is not where it starts. It starts as recognition. It starts as comfort. It starts as communion. It starts as a way of saying, *"I see you,"* without requiring a response. This is why touch is powerful for both men and women, even though they often experience it differently.

Many husbands do not crave sex as urgently as people assume; they crave being wanted. They crave initiation. They crave the feeling of being chosen again, not as an obligation but as a delight. Many wives do not crave sex as urgently as people assume; they crave safety. They crave attunement. They crave the feeling that their body is not just useful or attractive, but welcomed without demand. Neither desire is shallow. Both are sacred.

And this is where covenant matters. Covenant turns touch into belonging. It turns affection into recognition. It turns sexual intimacy into communion. Without a covenant, touch becomes negotiation. With the covenant, touch becomes renewal.

When the Apostle Paul wrote that husbands should love their wives as their own bodies, he assumed something we forgot: that bodies are not accessories to marriage; they are participants in the covenant. When Jesus healed, He touched more often than He preached.

Embodied grace is not a metaphor in Scripture; it is a ministry strategy. God does not save souls while ignoring bodies. He redeems both.

Touch Keeps Marriages Alive

Affection keeps marriages from becoming efficient partnerships. Communication keeps marriages from becoming cold contracts. Sex keeps marriages from becoming friendships without fire. But touch, the simple, ordinary, non-demanding kind, is what keeps bodies from drifting into separate worlds. It is the language spouses speak when words are not enough, and silence feels too far.

The Loss of Touch in High-Responsibility Seasons

Touch is often the first thing to disappear when marriages enter high-responsibility seasons. Not because love has diminished, but because bodies are busy. Children climb on them, work demands them, ministry pulls on them, and schedules commandeer them. By the time evening arrives, the body is no longer a place of invitation; it has become a place of fatigue. And fatigue rarely initiates tenderness. Fatigue doesn't just drain energy; it drains capacity for attunement.

The Role of Safety in Touch

Attunement requires presence, and presence is expensive when the nervous system has been running on fumes all day.

In attachment language, touch is one of the primary regulators of the body's stress response. A touch on the arm can lower heart rate, soften breathing, and communicate, *"You are not alone in this moment."* Most spouses do not realize they are attempting to build intimacy on top of a dysregulated nervous system. Dysregulated bodies are not rejecting affection; they are protecting themselves from overwhelm.

When couples understand this, contact stops feeling one-sided. The spouse who desires touch stops reading avoidance as rejection, and the spouse who avoids touch stops reading pursuit as demand. Many conflicts over sex, affection, and closeness are actually conflicts over regulation. One spouse wants to connect; the other wants to calm down. Neither is wrong. Both are unspoken.

Attachment Theory and Intimacy

Attachment theory names three core questions the body asks in intimate relationships:

1. *Are you here?* (presence)

2. *Are you with me?* (attunement)

3. *Do I matter?* (belonging)

Touch answers all three without requiring verbal explanation. A hand on the thigh during traffic communicates presence. A kiss on the cheek communicates attunement.

A lingering embrace communicates belonging. These gestures are small, but they are not trivial. They are the architecture of safety.

Family Influence on Touch

Family of origin shapes how easily these gestures are given and received. Some household's express affection freely; children climb into laps, siblings tackle one another, and parents hug in the kitchen.

Other households run on emotional minimalism. Physical proximity is functional, buckling seatbelts, passing dishes, washing hair, but not tender. In those homes, bodies are useful, not expressive. A child raised in a minimal-affection home may enter adulthood able to respect a spouse deeply but unable to interpret or initiate affectionate touch without anxiety or confusion.

Cultural and Religious Influence on Touch

Church culture can compound this. In some communities, the body is treated as a liability; something to be managed, controlled, and sanctified by distance. It is rarely treated as an instrument of grace. But Scripture never treats bodies as obstacles to holiness. The Incarnation contradicts that.

God does not save souls while ignoring bodies; He becomes a body and uses His own to heal the bodies of others. When Jesus restored dignity, He often did it through touch—hands on eyes, hands on lepers, hands on the dead. He could have spoken healing from a distance, and sometimes He did. But often, He chose proximity.

When an adult spouse has had affection withheld, weaponized, hyper-sexualized, or over-spiritualized, the nervous system may interpret touch as threat rather than comfort. Threat does not always look like fear; sometimes it looks like withdrawal, dismissal, or numbness. Numbness is not the absence of feeling; it is an overwhelming feeling. When Keisha withdrew after long days, she was not rejecting Andre; she was regulating. But because they had never named this dynamic, Andre interpreted regulation as disinterest. Misinterpretation is where marriages begin to create unnecessary pain. Comfortable touch cannot grow in environments of misinterpretation. It grows in environments of naming.

When spouses can say, *"I need your presence but not your pursuit right now,"* safety increases. When spouses can say, *"I need pursuit, not distance,"* clarity increases. Safety and clarity equal capacity for affection. Without those two ingredients, touch becomes a negotiation instead of a gift. Children model this effortlessly. A child climbs onto a parent's lap not to seduce or to earn approval but to regulate.

Adults forget this. We replace climbing with tasks. We replace presence with problem-solving. We replace attunement with advice. Advice may solve problems, but it rarely calms nervous systems. Many marriages are full of advice and efficient solutions but starved for comfort. Comfort is the invisible love language beneath all five love languages.

The Role of Touch in Intimacy

Regulated bodies receive affection more easily. Dysregulated bodies often recoil, not out of rejection but out of survival. The pastoral implication is profound: many marriages are not touch-starved because they lack love but because they lack peace. Peace makes room for presence. Presence makes room for affection. Affection makes room for desire. When desire grows out of safety, it is not frantic. It is not demanding. It is not transactional.

It is not self-conscious. It is spacious. *Spacious desire* is the soil in which long-term eroticism thrives. This is why older couples who have learned comfort often report deeper intimacy than couples in their twenties. They do not have the energy they once had, but they have something young people cannot manufacture—calm bodies that enjoy one another without fear. But tenderness is not optional for intimacy. Tenderness is the doorway. Many couples misunderstand this.

They treat touch as either foreplay or obligation. But most touch in marriage should be neither. It should be comfort. Comfort requires no performance and makes no demand. It communicates presence without pressure. *"I don't need sex,"* one wife told me, *"I need you to sit next to me without scrolling your phone."* Her husband didn't lack desire; he lacked attunement. Attunement is the ability to notice. *Notice subtlety. Notice mood. Notice longing.* Many marriages are not missing love; they are missing noticing. Men and women often experience touch differently, but not in the stereotypical way we've been taught. It is easy to assume men want sexual touch and women want emotional touch, but the truth is more layered. Many men crave non-sexual touch because it allows them to experience connection without having to initiate sexual pursuit.

Many women crave sexual touch because it allows them to experience being desired rather than merely being appreciated. Bodies are not predictable scripts; they are storied landscapes. Touch in marriage must learn to speak multiple dialects: comfort, playfulness, affection, desire, reassurance, curiosity, and rest. When touch only speaks the sexual dialect, it becomes a negotiation.

When it only speaks the comforting dialect, it becomes parental. When it only speaks the playful dialect, it becomes adolescent. Healthy marriages learn to speak them all.

The Return of Tenderness

This is why the return of touch after sexual intimacy has been restored is so important. Sex can reignite desire, but touch sustains belonging. Belonging is the soil in which desire grows without panic. Panic is the enemy of desire. When spouses begin to feel they must perform to keep the other satisfied, the body tenses, and tense bodies do not receive affection; they defend against it.

Keisha noticed this in herself before she ever named it. Sex had returned, and it was good. It was more relaxed, less pressured, less tense than before. But afterward, an old script returned: get up, clean up, move on. She didn't dislike Andre. She didn't avoid him.

She simply resumed efficiency. Andre didn't complain, but something in him sagged. Tenderness after intimacy is not an afterthought; it is part of the act. It is the body saying, *"Don't retreat yet. Stay here a little longer."*

For many husbands, post-sex tenderness is the only time their bodies are held without expectation. For many wives, pre-sex tenderness is the only time their bodies are pursued without demand. When a couple learns to hold one another before and after intimacy, they begin to close the loop on affection. Bodies learn the rhythm of approach and rest.

This is why the Song of Songs is full of hands, cheeks, necks, shoulders, lips, and hair. It is not merely a sexual poem; it is an embodied one. The lovers do not only admire one another; they touch one another. They anoint each other with oils, hold each other, lean into one another, frame one another with their gaze. The body is not a tool in that poem; it is a participant in the relationship.

The loss of non-sexual touch in marriage is often a sign that bodies have become functional and efficient, but not intimate. Efficiency is useful for building households, but intimacy is required for building a marriage. Many couples optimize schedules and productivity at the expense of affection and then wonder why their intimacy feels brittle or transactional. The body does not respond to efficiency the way the soul does. The body responds to presence.

Presence is not simply being in the same room. Presence is attention. It is noticing without fixing. It is curiosity without interrogation. It is warmth without strategy. Presence is the most erotic thing about long-term marriages. Not erotic in the pornified sense of arousal, but in the biblical sense of delight. Delight is what makes touch covenantal. It is what turns the body into a place of honor rather than shame. Jesus touched lepers not because He needed to, but because they needed to.

His touch restored dignity before it restored health. Marriage must learn that order. Touch restores dignity. Dignity restores safety. Safety restores desire. Desire restores intimacy. Intimacy restores the covenant. Covenant restores tenderness. And tenderness is what keeps marriage from leaking affection into silence.

Small Gestures in Touch

Keisha began experimenting with small gestures. Not sexual ones. Just human ones. When Andre walked past her in the kitchen, she let her hand rest on his shoulder for two extra seconds.

When they sat on the couch, she let her knee touch his instead of folding her legs away. When they prayed at night, she kept her hand in his instead of disengaging the moment *"amen"* was spoken.

None of these gestures required great intention. But they required attention. And attention is what bodies read.

Andre noticed, but he didn't pounce on the change. The old him would have interpreted touch as an invitation to escalate.

The mature man understood that affection could be a destination, not merely a doorway. So, he responded with equal gentleness: a kiss on the temple when she poured her coffee, a hand at the small of her back when they walked into church, a head leaned against hers during worship. Bodies learn new languages slowly, but they remember them quickly when the environment is safe.

Touch in Long-Term Marriages

Not every couple finds touch easy. Some grew up in homes where affection was scarce. Others had touch weaponized against them through violation, control, or premature exposure. Some learned that bodies exist for utility, not delight. Some over-intellectualized intimacy. Some over-spiritualize desire. Some were taught that holy marriages do not need physical affection, as if holiness is proved by distance. But holiness is not distance.

Holiness is alignment. Bodies aligned with covenant do not become less affectionate; they become more tender.

Playfulness in Touch

Touch also carries a playful dialect. Playfulness is a marker of safety. When marriages lose play, they often lose delight. And when delight disappears, sex becomes functional, affectionate touch becomes rare, and communication becomes transactional.

Play is not childish; it is courage without self-consciousness. Play is how adults signal, *"I am not threatened here."*

Playfulness often disappears from marriage long before sex does. Not because couples don't love each other, but because self-consciousness begins to replace curiosity. The body that once reached freely now waits for permission. The body that once flirted now calculates. But flirtation is not immaturity; it is desire without shame. It is how lovers signal, *"I still enjoy you."*

When couples lose play, they often lose delight. Delight is the fuel of long-term eroticism. Eroticism here does not mean explicit sexuality; it means the experience of one another as both familiar and intriguing. It is the paradox lovers navigate: *"I know you deeply, yet I can still discover you."* When discovery dies, eroticism dries up. Playfulness keeps discovery alive.

Many couples do not realize how much their dating years were held together by play. They teased. They stole kisses in cars. They whispered jokes in public. They touched each other's clothing. They sat too close in restaurants. These were not merely hormones. They were embodiments of curiosity. Curiosity is the opposite of complacency. Complacency is not the enemy of passion; assumption is. Passion does not require novelty; it requires attention.

The Song of Songs as a Model

Song of Songs is full of playful affection. The lovers do not merely admire each other's beauty; they delight in one another's bodies as landscapes. *"Your hair is like a flock of goats,"* may not sound poetic to modern ears, but to an ancient shepherd, it was flirtation. *"Your lips drip sweetness as the honeycomb," "Your scent is like Lebanon," "Your cheeks are lovely with ornaments."* These are not functional descriptions; they are delightful ones. The lovers are not efficient; they are enchanted.

Many Christian marriages unintentionally starve delight by over-spiritualizing intimacy. They treat the body as if holiness requires distance. But holiness does not shrink desire; it sanctifies it. Sanctified desire is not embarrassed by play. It does not apologize for delight. It does not feel guilty for wanting to be enjoyed.

It does not reduce sex to duty or affection to charity. It sees the spouse not as a responsibility but as a gift.

Covenant and Playfulness

Playfulness also disrupts the seriousness that life accumulates. Mortgages, ministry, aging parents, careers, children, and crises do not permit couples to flirt. Flirtation must be chosen against the gravity of responsibility.

A wife flicks water at her husband at the sink. A husband sways his wife in the kitchen for three seconds of dance. A spouse squeezes the other's thigh in the car at a red light.

These gestures are not childish; they are covenantal. They remind the body that marriage is not merely a partnership; it is a romance.

When couples rediscover play, they often rediscover desire. But the order matters: desire flows more easily out of delight than duty. Duty may sustain the outward structure of marriage, but delight sustains the inward joy. Joy is not trivial in a covenant. Scripture describes marriage as a place of joy, feasting, laughter, and blessing. If the gospel promises fullness of joy, what makes us believe marriage should settle for tolerable companionship?

Playfulness also repairs resentment more gently than argument. Arguments demand resolution; play invites presence. Presence often accomplishes what argument cannot.

A husband once told me, *"We were in a rough spot. Nothing I said worked. Then one day, I put a gummy bear on her shoulder without saying anything. She looked at me like I was insane and burst out laughing. It was the first time we laughed in months."* Laughter re-humanizes the spouse. Resentment de-humanizes them. The quickest way to remember that your spouse is not your adversary is to laugh together.

Some spouses fear playfulness because they fear rejection. Rejection wounds play more deeply than sexual wounds. Sexual rejection can feel like desire unanswered.

Playful rejection can feel like self-exposed. This is why couples must learn to receive play gently, without critique or sarcasm. Sarcasm poisons delight because it weaponizes vulnerability. Playfulness requires a soft landing.

In long-term marriages, playful touch becomes its own dialect. A hand brushed across the lower back. A finger traced along a forearm. Toes touching under blankets. A grabbed the belt loop in the hallway. A kiss on the shoulder while passing.

None of these gestures demands escalation. They communicate, *"I'm still here, and I still enjoy you."* Enjoyment is the fuel of covenantal passion. Without enjoyment, passion exhausts itself.

Andre discovered this one evening while washing dishes. Keisha walked up behind him and drew a line down his spine with one finger, stopping at his waistband. He froze, not with fear, but with intrigue. She laughed softly and walked away without explanation. It wasn't flirtation for sex; it was flirtation for delight. That gesture did more for their marriage that week than any strategy or date night. It reminded them both that a covenant does not flatten romance; it frees it from insecurity.

Even older couples rediscover this. A husband in his seventies once told me, *"My wife and I hold hands again. Not because we're frail, but because we remember."* When I asked what they remembered, he said, *"We remember that we are lovers, not just roommates who raised children together."* He said this without embarrassment. It was the most dignified thing in the room.

The Role of Touch and Presence in Covenant

Bodies are not incidental to the covenant. When God formed the first marriage, He did not join two souls in an abstract spiritual sense and then add bodies as accessories.

He formed Adam from the dust of the ground and breathed into his nostrils. He formed Eve from Adam's own flesh. The first words Adam spoke when he saw her were not philosophical; they were embodied: *"Bone of my bones and flesh of my flesh."* He did not speak first of companionship, ministry partnership, or shared assignment. He spoke of bodies belonging. *Covenant* is the context where bodies are allowed to be unashamed.

When sin entered, the first instinct was not to flee God intellectually but to hide physically. Shame expressed itself as bodily concealment. The problem was not nudity; the problem was unguarded exposure without safety. God's response was not to shame their bodies but to clothe them. Clothing was not punishment; it was mercy.

It allowed them to stay in a relationship while healing the fracture of shame. Many couples move through marriage with the same dynamic: longing for closeness, hiding behind fig leaves of competence, piety, or exhaustion, waiting for the covenant to make safety feel possible again.

Jesus continued this embodied pattern. The *Incarnation* was not God sampling human experience from a distance; it was God assuming a body that could be touched, held, kissed, pierced, and raised. Salvation was not a disembodied transaction; it was a bodily act.

Jesus healed the sick by touching them. He restored sight by touching the eyes. He blessed children by laying hands on them. He allowed a sinful woman to wipe His feet with her hair and tears. He allowed His body to be broken and offered for others. The gospel is not allergic to touch; it requires it.

Marriage is one of the few covenants where bodies remain central throughout the entire duration of the relationship. Bodies change across the decades; pregnancy, aging, illness, weight gain, weight loss, injury, stretch marks, scars. *Covenant* is what prevents those changes from becoming sources of shame. Touch is how covenant speaks dignity to changing bodies. A kiss on a scar says, *"You are still mine."* A hand on a softer waist says, *"I still delight in you."* Covenant does not freeze bodies in time; it blesses them in every season.

For some spouses, theology liberated their understanding of touch. They had been told that holiness required restraint but had never been taught that restraint is meant to serve delight, not eliminate it. They had been told that sex was for procreation or marital duty, but not for communion, laughter, curiosity, and feast. *Song of Songs* does not apologize for erotic joy. It sanctifies it. The beloved says, *"His left hand is under my head, and his right arm embraces me."* That is affection in Scripture; unhurried, unashamed, and unafraid.

The Healing Power of Affection

When couples recover the dignity of touch, they often experience healing that no amount of talking could accomplish. Words can explain; touch can restore. Words can clarify; touch can reconcile. Words can negotiate; touch can mend. This is why many couples report that the breakthrough in their marriage did not happen in counseling sessions but afterward—in the car, on the couch, or in the kitchen, when one spouse finally reached out without expectation or agenda. That gesture said what their vocabulary could not: *"You are safe with me."* Affection in covenant is sacramental, not in the technical theological sense, but in the experiential one. It is an outward sign of an inward grace.

It reveals the invisible bond of belonging visibly and tangibly. If *Communion* nourishes the soul, affectionate touch nourishes the marriage. It keeps the covenant from becoming conceptual. It keeps intimacy from becoming theoretical. It keeps love from becoming disembodied.

Reflection is how marriages notice. Activation is how marriages rehearse. Prayer is how marriages surrender. A declaration is how marriages align. Affection is how marriages remember.

Reflection

Sit with these questions gently, without analysis or blame:

1. Where has affection grown quiet in our marriage?
2. What has our touch been saying without words?
3. Which dialects of touch did we lose: comfort, play, desire, reassurance?
4. What did I learn about touch from my family growing up?
5. How easy is it for me to receive touch without performing?
6. How easy is it for me to give touch without demanding?

Activation

For the next seven days, engage in non-sexual, affectionate touch once per day. Not for negotiation. Not for escalation. Simply for belonging.

Examples include:

- Sitting close without an agenda
- Unhurried hugs

- Hand-holding in public or in prayer
- Shoulder-to-shoulder conversations
- Temple kisses
- Feet touching beneath blankets
- Hands in hair
- Palm on back during worship

If sexual intimacy follows, celebrate it; if it doesn't, don't interpret it. *Affection is not foreplay.* Affection is covenant glue.

Prayer

Lord, You formed our bodies with intention and placed us in covenant so we could be known without fear. Restore tenderness where fatigue has settled, restore delight where heaviness has lived, and restore safety where distance has grown. Teach our bodies to relax in one another's presence and to speak affectionately without pressure. Let touch become communion and belonging in our marriage. In Jesus' name, Amen.

Declaration (Spouse to Spouse)

I touch you not to demand anything, but to remember us. I choose tenderness over tension, and affection over avoidance. Your body is not my entitlement; it is my companion in covenant.

Affirmation (Personal)

I am allowed to desire tenderness. I am allowed to enjoy playfulness. My body is a participant in the covenant, not an accessory to it. Affection is holy.

***

Touch sustains intimacy, but even tenderness requires maintenance. Without intentional renewal, connections can grow dry under the weight of routine and responsibility. What is not replenished will eventually weaken.

***

Chapter 11

Re-Oiling The Marriage

***

There are two kinds of breakdowns in marriage: the catastrophic and the gradual. Catastrophic breakdowns are dramatic, an affair, a betrayal, a crisis, a revelation. Everyone can see when the engine seizes, and smoke pours out from under the hood. But most marriages do not fail catastrophically; they dry out gradually. They run out of oil, not love. Oil is what keeps friction from becoming damage.

Andre and Keisha learned this the slow way. After years of ministry, parenting, and chasing bills, their marriage did not explode; it simply became noisy. Every disagreement felt louder. Every request felt heavier. Every inconvenience became an argument. Nothing had happened, and yet everything felt harder. When Andre finally took his car for an overdue oil change, the mechanic told him, *"You're lucky. You were close to metal on metal."* He laughed it off at the time. Months later, he would sit across from Keisha on the couch and say, *"I think our marriage feels like it's metal on metal."*

Cars don't run without lubrication, and marriages don't either. Oil is what allows machines to handle pressure without seizing up. Wiper fluid keeps the windshield clear so you can see. Grease keeps hinges from grinding. None of these products fix engines or rebuild transmissions. They do something more important: they maintain motion.

Most couples underestimate how much routine maintenance their marriage requires. Not because they don't care, but because they assume love should stay smooth on its own. But nothing stays smooth on its own; not cars, not bodies, not faith, not friendships, and certainly not marriages. Anything under pressure must be tended. Anything exposed to the elements must be maintained. Anything valuable must be oiled.

The First Sign of Dryness

The first sign of dryness in marriage is not silence or distance; it is friction. Friction sounds like shortness, sighs, sarcasm, huffs, rolled eyes, interruptions, and impatience. Friction feels like pushing, grinding, defending, and overreacting. Friction is not hatred; friction is effort without lubrication. Oil is what allows love to move without losing gentleness.

Marriages do not become rigid because couples stop loving each other. They become rigid because they stop pursuing each other. Pursuit is the oil of the covenant. It is the consistent decision to tend to the relationship rather than assume it will tend to itself. Machines demand lubrication; marriages demand attention. Attention is not the same as intensity. Many couples try to rescue dryness with intensity; big trips, big gifts, big apologies. But dryness is rarely healed by intensity. Dryness heals through rhythm. It heals through the slow return of small choices that say, *"I still see you. I still choose you. I am still learning you."*

Oil as a Symbol in Scripture

Scripture often treats oil as a symbol of consecration, joy, healing, and preparation. Kings were anointed with oil. Priests were consecrated with oil. Wounds were soothed with oil. Lamps were fueled with oil. The beloved in the *Song of Songs* described her lover's very name as "oil poured out." Oil was never simply decorative; it was functional. It kept things burning, moving, healing, and shining. Marriage needs all four functions.

- It needs consecration—*"We belong to God and to each other."*
- It needs joy—*"We are not just roommates; we are lovers."*

- It needs healing—*"We do not let wounds linger."*
- It needs fuel—*"We keep the light burning."*

When any of these functions dry up, friction increases. When they dry up long enough, the marriage begins to stall. And when stalling becomes normal, couples begin to interpret dryness as incompatibility instead of neglect. Neglect is rarely intentional. It is almost always the byproduct of pressure. Pressure from children. Pressure from work. Pressure from the ministry. Pressure from aging parents. Pressure from finances. Pressure from expectations. Under pressure, couples begin to conserve energy. They stop pursuing and start maintaining. Maintenance is not sinful; it is simply insufficient. Marriages need maintenance, but they cannot survive on maintenance alone. Lovers must become maintenance workers, but maintenance workers must remain lovers.

Dryness in Marriage: Not Always Obvious

Keisha once assumed that Andre's lack of pursuit meant he wasn't interested. But when she asked him, he said, *"I'm tired. I don't know how to pursue you and survive life at the same time."* Many husbands feel this long before they can name it. Pursuit feels risky. Maintenance feels safe. But maintenance is not oiling.

Maintenance is merely preventing collapse. Oiling is what keeps the engine humming.

Dryness in marriage is not always dramatic. Sometimes it is subtle, married couples sitting at the same dinner table scrolling on separate screens. Sleeping back-to-back with a foot of mattress between them and eating in silence and praying without touching, and serving at church without watching each other, and living side-by-side without delight. Delight is the first fluid to leak when life becomes heavy. But delight can be replenished. Oil can be topped up. The marriage does not need a new engine; it needs lubrication.

Spouses often wait for the other to initiate the oil change. *"When she starts being affectionate, I'll start pursuing." "When he starts pursuing, I'll start opening up."* But stalemates do not produce lubrication. Stalemates produce stalling. Someone must choose movement first. Someone must pour oil where the relationship has dried. In spiritual life, oil is often applied before motion. Lamps were filled with oil before nightfall. Priests were anointed before service. Kings were anointed before their coronation. Wounds were treated with oil before bandages. Oil was never an afterthought; it was preparation. Couples often attempt motion without preparation and wonder why everything feels heavy.

Re-oiling the Marriage

Re-oiling the marriage is about reintroducing the rhythms that make movement smooth again. Rhythms of noticing. Rhythms of pursuing. Rhythms of tending. Rhythms of honoring.

These rhythms do not eliminate friction; they prevent friction from becoming damage.

Andre learned this one evening while they were washing dishes. Keisha bumped him with her hip, nothing sexual, nothing dramatic, just playful weight. He bumped her back. She flicked water at him and laughed. He took the dishtowel and snapped it gently in her direction. She shrieked, half-offended and half-delighted. It lasted less than ten seconds, but something loosened. They had not played in years. Oil returned in a flick of water and a dishtowel. Motion became easier. The kitchen felt lighter.

Marriages rarely need rescue as much as they need oil. Rescue is for emergencies. Oil is for ordinary life. Oil in Scripture is never neutral. Oil marks transitions. Oil marks callings. Oil marks joy. Oil marks healing. Oil marks preparation. When a king was anointed, oil was poured, not dabbed. When wounds were treated, oil was applied, not suggested. When lamps were lit, oil burned, not merely stored. Oil is always active.

It exists to make movement possible. When David wrote of oil running down the head and beard of the priest, it was not about grooming; it was about overflow. Blessing was not merely internal; it was messy, fragrant, visible, and communal. Anyone near the priest could smell it.

Oil announced, *"Something sacred is happening here."* Marriage needs that kind of oil. Not polite love. Not invisible affection. Not whispered duty. Overflow.

Marriage dries out when affection becomes polite, pursuit becomes optional, and delight becomes nostalgic. Nostalgia is a sign that oil is low. When couples speak more fondly of what they used to be than what they are becoming, dryness has already set in. Nostalgia can be inspiring for a season, but it becomes depressing when it replaces movement. Dry marriages talk about memories; oiled marriages talk about possibilities.

Oil also has a healing function. When the Samaritan encountered the wounded man on the road, he did not pray from a distance. He poured oil on his wounds. Oil was a treatment, not a sermon. Many marriages attempt to heal wounds with lectures or apologies. Apologies matter, but apologies without tenderness often feel like receipts. Oil makes the apology believable. Oil restores dignity before it restores function.

The Oil of Joy

There is also the *oil of joy*. Isaiah describes God granting "the oil of gladness instead of mourning." The text assumes that joy is not merely a feeling but something that can be bestowed. In marriage, joy is one of the most potent oils.

Joy is what makes affection playful rather than dutiful. *Joy* is what makes sex desirable rather than stressful. *Joy* is what makes communication safe rather than strategic. *Joy* is not frivolous. *Joy* lubricates covenant.

Keisha did not realize how little joy she carried into their marriage until one evening she watched another couple laugh at a restaurant. They weren't flirting, and they weren't making jokes. They were simply enjoying being together. She saw the way the woman touched the man's forearm absentmindedly. The way he rested his hand on the back of her neck. Nothing sexual. Everything soft. "They look like they like each other," Keisha whispered. It startled her when she stopped liking Andre. She loved him fiercely. She respected him deeply. But *like*? *Like* had dried. Marriage is built on love, but marriage survives on *love*. *Oil* restores *like*.

Then there is the *oil of preparation*. In ancient households, brides were perfumed and anointed before the wedding ceremony. Love was not left to chance; it was prepared for.

Even Jesus' parable of the ten virgins revolves around oil: some carried enough to sustain the wait, and others assumed the wait would be short. Marriage is closer to that parable than most couples admit.

Desire does not disappear because of the lack of love. It disappears because of the lack of *oil*. Preparation sustains desire when circumstances delay fulfillment.

Andre assumed that romance would simply reignite once their circumstances settled down. But circumstances rarely settle; they rearrange. Children change into adolescents. Careers plateau or accelerate. Aging parents need care. Hormones fluctuate. Seasons shift. *Oil* is what keeps romance from becoming seasonal. When romance depends on the season, winter becomes dangerous.

Oil also has a deeply embodied dimension. It softens surfaces. It soothes skin. It reduces friction. It creates glide. Flour, spices, or salt enhance flavor, but *oil* creates texture. Without *oil*, even the best ingredients in the pan will burn. Without *oil*, marriages with excellent ingredients, shared values, faith, attraction, and compatibility, can still scorch under pressure.

This is why sexual intimacy appears in the Song not merely as passion but as fragrance and *oil*. "Your name is *oil* poured out," the beloved says. Name here means identity, presence, and reputation. *Oil* poured out suggests generosity.

Lovers in covenant are meant to be generous with pursuit, affection, attention, and delight. When pursuit dries, covenant becomes competent but not captivating.

Competent marriages are often the most dangerously dry.

They pay bills.
They raise children.
They tithe.
They serve.
They sleep in the same bed.
They attend church.
They lead Bible studies.

Everything works.

But they do not oil.
They do not surprise.

They do not pursue.

They do not play.

They do not touch.

They do not delight.

They are faithful, but frictional.

They are holy, but humorless.

They are united, but un-oiled.

Re-oiling requires attention. Attention is not the same as analysis. Analysis dissects; attention beholds. When a husband studies his wife without trying to fix her, he *oils* her. When a wife notices her husband's efforts without critiquing his strategy, she *oils* him. Attention is the first anointing of any relationship.

Attention then becomes action. Action becomes pursuit. Pursuit becomes rhythm. Rhythm becomes culture. Culture becomes ease. Ease is the opposite of dryness. Ease is not laziness; it is glide. Glide is what marriages were designed for. Not frictionless perfection, but smooth recovery. Smooth reconnection. Smooth delight.

Andre and Keisha began to re-oil in small ways. Andre started watching Keisha get ready for church, not lustfully, but attentively. He noticed the way she layered her necklaces, the way she brushed her hair behind her ear, the way she checked her teeth before walking out the door. "You look beautiful," he said one Sunday morning, not as a compliment but as an observation. Keisha felt *oiled.* She reached out and adjusted his collar. "So do you," she smiled.

Oil is contagious. *Oil* becomes a rhythm, not a rescue. Rescue is what couples reach for when the marriage has stalled. *Oil* is what couples use to keep the motion smooth before stalling ever occurs. Every marriage needs three kinds of *oiling*: daily oils, weekly oils, and seasonal oils.

Daily oils are small, almost invisible gestures that keep affection alive. They do not take time; they take noticing.

A text in the middle of the day. A kiss before leaving the house. A hand on the back during worship. Sitting together on the couch instead of opposite ends of the room. Laughter in the kitchen. A compliment that is not required. A prayer that includes the spouse's actual need rather than generic petitions. None of these gestures demands a date night, a vacation, or a counseling appointment. They simply require attention. Attention is the smallest unit of *oil.*

Weekly oils require intention. They are the choices that say, "We invest in us." This can be a meal out, a planned walk, a shared coffee, a hobby enjoyed side-by-side, or a Sabbath-style pause in the week.

Weekly oils need not be sexual, though sexual intimacy can be one of them. The point of weekly oils is not entertainment; it is a pursuit. Pursuit is the ingredient of intimacy that cannot be automated. It must be chosen. When pursuit becomes predictable, marriages stop wondering. When marriages stop wondering, desire goes dormant.

Seasonal oils require foresight. These are the investments that say, "Our marriage is not a side project." A marriage retreat. A trip without children. A counseling intensive.

A spiritual pilgrimage. A family reset. A vacation with margin instead of obligation. Seasonal oils recalibrate the marriage for the next leg of the journey. They are to marriage what overhauls are to engines. Without them, small fractures become structural.

Couples often assume that daily oils compensate for the absence of seasonal oils or that seasonal oils compensate for the absence of daily oils. But *oiling* is cumulative. Daily oils keep friction low. Weekly oils keep the connection warm. Seasonal oils keep vision alive. If any one category dries out, the marriage becomes lopsided.

Andre and Keisha discovered this in reverse. For years, they had seasonal oil vacations, family trips, and ministry conferences without daily oils. They were competent travelers and excellent ministers, but they were poor pursuers.

Every trip was an attempt to recapture something that had not been tended during ordinary life. They would leave the country with expectations and return with disappointment. Not because the trip failed, but because the trip could not fix what dryness had slowly hardened at home.

Oil must be applied where friction exists, not where aesthetics is convenient. Marriages often polish what is visible and ignore what is grinding.

Re-oiling the marriage also requires forgiveness. Forgiveness is *oil* for the wounds caused by friction. Without forgiveness, friction becomes resentment. Resentment fossilizes. Fossils cannot be persuaded; they can only be broken.

Forgiveness softens what time hardens. It allows pursuit to resume. Forgiveness is not denial; it is lubrication for the soul.

Some couples hesitate to re-oil because they believe too much damage has already occurred. *Oil* cannot undo scratches on the metal, but it can prevent deeper scoring. Some couples hesitate because they believe everything is fine. *Oil* does not exist for broken engines; *oil* exists for engines that are running. The healthiest marriages are often the most oiled, not because they are in crisis but because they are in motion.

Oil is also sensual. It smooths surfaces, enhances glide, softens touch, and responds to heat. When Scripture likens intimacy to spices and *oils*, it is not using delicate imagery; it is using embodied language. Sexual desire dries out in marriages not merely from sin or conflict, but from lack of lubrication: physical, emotional, spiritual, and relational. *Oil* transitions the marriage from duty to delight.

Oil is also celebratory. In ancient times, guests were anointed with *oil* at feasts. Their faces shone.

Their heads glistened. *Oil* was part of honor, not necessity. Marriage needs this *oil* too. Honor is *oil*. Admiration is *oil*. Celebration is *oil*. Many marriages suffer from honor-scarcity. Spouses become mutual critics instead of mutual celebrants. *Oil* restores celebration.

Oil finally serves as preparation. Lamps must be filled before nightfall. Brides were perfumed before the wedding feast. Warriors were anointed before battle. Couples who wait for a crisis to prepare for intimacy will always *oil* too late.

Reflection

Pause and reflect without defensiveness:

1. Where has our marriage become mechanical?

2. Where has friction replaced glide?

3. Where have we depended on memory instead of pursuit?

4. Where has joy become nostalgic instead of current?

5. Where have we waited for the other to *oil* first?

Activation

For the next four weeks, choose one *oil* from each category:

- **Daily oil**: a form of attention (small, consistent)

- **Weekly oil**: a form of pursuit (shared presence)

- **Seasonal oil**: a form of investment (renewal)

- **Sacred oil**: a form of consecration (prayer and blessing)

Do not evaluate the results mid-week. *Oil* works gradually.

Prayer

Father, You anoint with oil, heal with oil, and sustain with oil.

Let our marriage be marked by joy, tenderness, pursuit, and honor. Restore what has dried. Heal what has cracked. Soften what has hardened. And let our covenant glide with grace.

In Jesus' name, Amen.

Declaration (Spouse to Spouse)

I do not only love you; I pursue you. I do not only stay; I delight.

I choose tenderness over tension, pursuit over passivity,

and *oil* over dryness.

Affirmation (Personal)

I am worth pursuit.

I am worth delight.

My marriage is worth oil.

***

Oil reduces friction, but communication interprets friction. Many couples are not fighting about sex, or touch, or oil; they are fighting about meaning. What did that sigh mean? What did that silence mean? What did that request mean? Communication is the sealant that keeps meaning from leaking into assumption.

***

Chapter 12

Communication: The Sealant Against Leaks

***

The argument did not begin with sin or betrayal. It began with a sigh. Keisha stood at the sink rinsing plates while Andre scrolled through his phone at the counter. The day had been long, with bills, ministry meetings, homework oversight, and a late grocery run. Nothing unusual. When Keisha reached for the dishwasher handle, and it refused to budge, she let out a sharp exhale without thinking. Andre looked up, startled.

"What was that supposed to mean?" he asked.

"Nothing," she said. But the word didn't land as nothing. It landed as something. He interpreted it as irritation. She interpreted his question as an accusation. Neither interpretation was spoken, but both shaped the conversation that followed.

Communication breakdowns rarely begin with words. They begin with interpretation. Most couples do not fight over what was said. They fight over what they think the other person meant.

Tone becomes meaning. Silence becomes meaning. Timing becomes meaning. Even sighs become meaningful. The dishwasher eventually opened, but their hearts did not. The conversation that followed had nothing to do with dishes. It had everything to do with longing. Longing to be understood. Longing to be appreciated and longing to be seen. Every marriage carries these longings. When they are met, marriages glide. When they leak, marriages grind.

Communication is the sealant that keeps longing from leaking into assumption. The Scriptures speak of words as if they have substance. Tongues are not merely instruments of sound; they are instruments of direction, power, and healing. Words can bless or curse, soothe or pierce, build or erode. In marriage, words do not merely convey information; they confer interpretation. Spouses interpret each other long before they understand each other. Communication is not merely about accuracy; it is about meaning-making. Two people can report the same facts and arrive at opposite meanings. *Meaning* is where covenant succeeds or collapses.

When love first begins, couples are often generous with interpretation. A forgotten call means, *"He must be busy."*

A delayed text means, *"She probably fell asleep."* But as marriages grow weary and oil runs low, interpretations shift. A forgotten call becomes, *"He doesn't care."* A delayed text becomes, *"She's ignoring me."*

The facts remain the same; the meaning changes. *Meaning* always reveals the state of the heart.

Communication in marriage is not simply the exchange of information; it is the exchange of interpretations. Two histories, two nervous systems, two vocabularies, and two sets of wounds all attempting to translate one relationship. When translation breaks down, leaks form. When leaks are not sealed, pressure increases. When pressure increases, friction rises. When friction rises without oil, marriages seize.

Keisha's sigh meant, *"I am tired and overwhelmed."* Andre's interpretation was, *"You are frustrated with me again."* Andre's question meant, *"Are we okay?"* Keisha's interpretation was, *"You are criticizing me again."* Neither intention was hostile, but both interpretations were defensive. And so, a simple moment became a complex meaning-negotiation without either spouse naming what they actually felt.

Communication breakdowns are less about expression and more about assumptions. Couples assume faster than they articulate.

They defend faster than they inquire. They retreat faster than they reveal. Silence becomes strategy. Sarcasm becomes armor. Volume becomes leverage. Distance becomes safety. Communication in marriage often fails in four predictable ways:

First: Silence

Silence is not always peaceful. Sometimes silence is avoidance. Silence says, *"Talking feels dangerous."* Silence also says, *"If I speak, you will not hear me."* Many spouses were formed in homes where silence was easier than honesty. Silence keeps the peace but forfeits intimacy. Peace without intimacy becomes coldness.

Second: Harshness

Harshness is not simply volume; it is tone. Tone often communicates fear before words do. Harsh tones say, *"I need control because I feel threatened."* Harsh tones activate defense in the other spouse, even when the content is reasonable. Two defensives cannot hear each other. Defensiveness turns communication into combat.

Third: Distraction

Distraction signals disinterest even when disinterest is not present. A spouse can love deeply and still become distracted by fatigue, work, ministry, or screens. Distraction communicates, *"You are not a priority,"* even when the heart means, *"I have no bandwidth."* Attention is a form of honor. Distraction is a form of absence.

Fourth: Fear

Fear is the most unspoken communication barrier. Fear of conflict. Fear of being misunderstood. Fear of being dismissed. Fear of being judged. Fear of being too much. Fear silences spouses not because they have nothing to say, but because they cannot risk being unheard. Fear turns longing into resentment, and resentment is longing that has stopped hoping.

Communication fails not because couples do not talk, but because couples do not reveal. Many spouses speak in coded language, hinting at needs rather than naming them. They ask for help with the dishes when what they really desire is partnership. They complain about phones when what they desire is attention. They argue about schedules when what they need is rest. They criticize spending habits when what they fear is scarcity. Communication becomes a battlefield for unspoken needs.

Andre once said to Keisha, *"You never listen."* But when we translate that statement through longing, it becomes, *"I don't feel considered."* Keisha once said to Andre, *"You don't care."* But through longing, it becomes, *"I want to matter to you."* Marriage becomes healthier when longing is spoken instead of accusation.

Longing is the language of intimacy. Accusation is the language of self-protection. Many couples never learn to speak longingly because they never learned that longing is allowed. Longing requires vulnerability, and vulnerability requires safety. Safety is the soil where communication grows. Communication, then, is not simply verbal. It is nervous system to nervous system. Presence to presence. Face to face. Tone to tone. Breath to breath. Spouses do not merely hear each other; they perceive each other. And perception can distort meaning long before clarity arrives.

Communication as a Sealant

This is why communication functions as a sealant in marriage. Sealants do not remove pressure; they prevent leaks. Pressure will come in marriage: financial pressure, parenting pressure, ministry pressure, sexual pressure, and emotional pressure. Pressure is neutral. Pressure reveals whether a sealant has been applied.

The sealant of marriage is not compatibility but communication. Compatibility may bring two people together, but communication keeps them together.

Compatibility can ignite romance, but communication sustains a covenant. Compatibility can create chemistry, but communication sustains commitment. Communication is the covenantal practice of saying, *"I am willing to understand you."* Understanding is the spiritual discipline of marriage. It requires curiosity. It requires humility. It requires slowing down. It requires listening without rehearsing rebuttals. It requires asking, *"What did you hear me say?"* instead of assuming the message landed as intended.

Couples who communicate well do not avoid conflict; they navigate conflict without hemorrhaging connection. Conflict is not the enemy of marriage. Disconnection is. Conflict can be repaired. Disconnection, when prolonged, becomes distance. Distance becomes detachment. Detachment becomes numbness. Numbness is harder to heal than conflict.

Andre and Keisha did not eliminate conflict. They eliminated leakage. When the leakage stopped, the pressure decreased.

When pressure decreased, tenderness returned. Tenderness became the new normal. Tenderness is the oil of communication.

Embodied Communication

Communication in marriage is not merely about words; it is about embodiment. Spouses do not communicate only through sentences; they communicate through breath, posture, gaze, and proximity. A spouse can say, *"I'm listening,"* but if their body is angled away, arms folded, eyes down, and breath shallow, the body preaches a different sermon. The nervous system does not lie.

Tone can betray content. Breath can betray tone. Bodies speak before mouths do. This is why emotional safety is not created through vocabulary but through presence. *Presence* is what makes vulnerability possible. *Vulnerability* is what makes intimacy possible. *Intimacy* is what makes a covenant meaningful. Marriage without presence becomes administrative.

Marriage with presence becomes relational. When spouses feel unsafe in communication, they do not stop speaking. They switch modes. Some escalate. Some withdraw. Some intellectualize. Some distract. Some joke. Some blame. Some spiritualize. All of these are forms of protective communication.

Protective communication preserves self but forfeits connection. Intimate communication risks self to form a connection.

Keisha grew up in a household where feelings were handled privately. Her mother would disappear into her bedroom when upset. Her father would busy himself with chores. No fights. No raised voices. No explanations. Just quiet. Andre grew up in a home where everything was verbalized immediately, sometimes loudly, sometimes clumsily, but honestly. Neither model was sinful, but neither was sufficient for the covenant. Covenant demands both honesty and tenderness. *Honesty* without *tenderness* wounds. *Tenderness* without *honesty* withholds.

These family-of-origin dynamics often collide in marriage. The spouse who learned silence interprets volume as a threat. The spouse who learned volume interprets silence as rejection. Neither interpretation is accurate, but both feel true in the body. The nervous system reacts faster than the mind can correct. Communication in marriage requires not only the renewal of the mind but the re-conditioning of the nervous system. This is where covenant communication differs from secular communication. Secular communication focuses on accuracy. Covenant communication focuses on meaning and belonging.

Accuracy matters, but accuracy without belonging becomes transactional. Marriage is not a debate to be won; it is a heart to be known.

This leads us to one of the most important dimensions of communication in marriage:

Communication is witnessing. When a spouse speaks, they are not merely reporting information; they are revealing inner worlds. To witness a spouse's inner world is to say, *"I see you, I hear you, and your interior life matters to me."* Covenant requires witnessing. Witnessing is what differentiates a spouse from a roommate. Roommates coordinate logistics. Covenants witness souls. Jesus functioned as a covenant witness in His earthly ministry.

He listened to what people said. He asked questions that revealed their hearts. *"What do you want me to do for you?"* He asked the blind man. *"Do you want to be well?"* He asked the man by the pool. He did not assume longing; he invited longing. *Longing* must be invited before it can be healed.

Spouses often assume longing without inviting it. Or worse, they suppress longing because it feels inconvenient. But longing is the engine of intimacy. When longing is silenced, intimacy dries. When longing is named, intimacy flows.

Communication is how longing becomes speakable. But longing alone is not enough. After longing is spoken, it must be interpreted, and after interpretation, it must be negotiated, and after negotiation, it must be honored. This process is what seals the marriage against leakage.

Understanding Longing in Communication

Most couples never reach negotiation because they get stuck at interpretation. *"You never help in the evenings"* is interpreted as an accusation instead of an invitation. *"You don't listen"* is interpreted as condemnation instead of longing. *"You're always distracted"* is interpreted as disrespect instead of desire for attention. Beneath every protest is *desire*. Desire is never sinful; it is unskilled longing. This is where repair attempts become holy.

Repair is not about erasing conflict. Repair is about restoring connection. In a covenant, the goal is not to win but to return.

There are three layers of repair that marriages must learn: emotional, clarifying, and covenantal.

Emotional Repair:

"I can see this hurt you."

"I didn't realize that landed that way."

"You matter to me, even right now."

This type of repair addresses the wound.

Clarifying Repair:

"What I meant was..."

"What I heard you say was..."

"Can we slow down and understand what just happened?"

This type of repair addresses the meaning.

Covenantal Repair:

"I am not leaving this conversation emotionally."

"We are still on the same team."

"Our marriage is bigger than this moment."

This type of repair addresses the belonging.

All three are necessary for communication to become seamless. If wounds are healed but belonging is uncertain, spouses communicate carefully out of fear. If meaning is clarified but wounds are untreated, spouses communicate accurately but without tenderness. If belonging is affirmed but nothing is clarified, spouses feel loved but remain confused.

Andre and Keisha had to learn this slowly. One afternoon, they argued about finances. The words were ordinary, overspending on groceries, surprise charges on the debit card, but the meanings were heavy. For Keisha, overspending meant responsibility. For Andre, surprise expenses meant incompetence. Neither interpretation was accurate, but both were real. Midway through the conversation, Keisha took a breath and said, *"Wait, what did you hear me say?"* Andre paused. *"I heard you say you don't trust me to make good choices."* Keisha blinked. *"That's not what I said. I was trying to say I feel alone in planning."* The conversation softened. Wounds were not erased, but leakage stopped. They had entered repair.

The Role of Communication in Marriage

Repair is not linear. It requires courage to ask, *"Did I get that right?"* It requires humility to say, *"I think I missed you."* It requires regulation to breathe, slow down, and resist the urge to defend. It requires honor to stay emotionally present. *Honor* is oil for communication.

The spiritual dimension of communication cannot be ignored. Communication is the means by which unity is preserved. Jesus prayed not for uniformity but for unity, oneness of heart, not sameness of opinion. Unity in marriage is not agreement; it is alignment. Alignment is when two lives move in the same direction, even when they do not always speak the same words. Communication finally becomes seamless when it is rhythmic. Spouses cannot rely solely on crisis communication.

Crisis communication is reactive. Rhythmic communication is preemptive. Rhythmic communication says, *"We talk before we leak."* Couples who develop rhythm do not wait for arguments to name inner worlds. They make space for revelation as a lifestyle.

Rhythms of communication prevent marriages from becoming reactive. Reactive communication waits for conflict, then tries to clean up the mess. Rhythmic communication creates space for transparency before friction becomes resentment. Many couples never develop communication rhythms because they assume that talking "just happens." Talking happens. *Understanding* does not. Understanding requires rhythm. Healthy marriages practice three key communication rhythms: daily check-in, weekly connection, and seasonal review.

Daily Check-In:

The daily check-in is brief and embodied. It may sound like:

"What was the emotional temperature of your day?"

"Where are you exhausted?"

"Where did you feel accomplished?"

"What do you need from me tonight, attention, help, silence, or affection?"

These are not interrogations; they are openings. They do not require deep analysis; they require presence. *Presence* is often enough.

Weekly Connection:

The weekly connection is longer. This is space for meaningful updates, plans, and shared inner worlds:

"What has been on your mind lately?"

"Where have you felt connected?"

"Where have you felt alone?"

"What has been worrying you?"

These questions move beyond logistics and into longing. *Logistics* are necessary; bills, schedules, tasks, ministry, but longing is what preserves oil.

Seasonal Review:

The seasonal review is reflective. Every few months, couples ask:

"How are we doing?"

"Where is communication leaking?"

"What is working?"

"What needs attention?"

"What do we want to build next?"

Seasonal reviews are not autopsies; they are adjustments. Couples who review seasonally avoid drifting. Drifting is what dries marriages more than conflict.

Communication rhythms also allow spouses to recalibrate expectations. Many arguments are simply collisions between unspoken expectations. Expectations are not sinful; unspoken expectations are. When expectations go unspoken, spouses assume disinterest or disrespect.

When spoken, expectations become agreements or negotiations. Negotiation is not compromise; negotiation is collaboration.

Andre once believed that communication required speeches. Keisha believed communication required intuition. Neither was fully right. Covenantal communication requires clarity. *Clarity* is the antidote to assumption.

When couples communicate clearly, they reduce the amount of mental interpretation required. *Interpretation* uses emotional energy. *Clarity* preserves it.

The Role of Prayer in Communication

Communication also becomes sealant through prayer, not as a spiritual bypass, but as a form of belonging.

When couples pray together, they are not merely asking God to fix problems; they are practicing mutual surrender. Surrender is not passive; surrender is alignment. Prayer realigns hearts to God, and aligned hearts interpret one another more generously. *Generosity* is lubrication for meaning. Prayer does not replace communication; it softens communication. Spouses who pray together often listen differently. They assume differently. They approach differently. They repent differently. They heal differently. Prayer turns accusation into intercession.

It is difficult to demonize someone you are actively interceding for. But prayer must not be weaponized. Weaponized prayer sounds like, *"Lord, help my spouse see how wrong they are."* Weaponized prayer pretends to surrender while demanding victory. *Covenant* prayer says, *"Lord, soften me first."* Softened hearts communicate without knives. Hardened hearts communicate with blades.

Safety in Communication

Some couples avoid communication because they have been wounded in it. Words became sharp. Tone became hostile. Silence became punishment. Distance became defense. For these marriages, the first step is not learning to speak but learning to feel safe again. Safety may begin with counseling.

Safety may begin with boundaries. Safety may begin with an apology. Safety may begin with slowing down. But safety must begin.

Communication is not merely a skill; it is a ministry. To communicate with your spouse is to minister to their inner world. Ministers listen for meaning. Ministers attend to wounds. Ministers honor the soul. Marriage is not merely romantic; it is priestly. Husbands and wives are priests to one another's hearts. Priests do not always fix. Priests witness, anoint, and accompany.

Andre learned priestly communication slowly. One evening after a tense conversation, Keisha sat on the couch and stared at the wall. The old Andre would have walked away, assuming silence meant avoidance. The new Andre sat beside her and said, *"I'm here whenever you're ready."* He did not pry, he did not push, he did not perform. He witnessed. Minutes later, Keisha exhaled. *"I'm not mad,"* she said. *"I'm scared."* Fear had been the meaning behind the sigh. Fear had been the meaning behind the sharpness. Fear had been the meaning behind the distance. They had not been fighting about groceries. They had been fighting about fear.

Communication becomes easier when fear is named. *Fear* unspoken becomes anger. *Anger* unexamined becomes bitterness. *Bitterness* unaddressed becomes numbness. *Numbness* is the hardest condition to treat in marriage. Couples can work with anger; numbness removes hope. Communication is the tool that reaches numb hearts.

Communication finally becomes sealant when it combines clarity and tenderness, repair, and belonging. When these converge, marriages become drip-free.

Reflection

Sit with these questions gently, without analyzing your spouse:

- Where do I assume instead of asking?
- Where do I defend instead of reveal?
- Where do I react instead of repair?
- Where does fear shape my communication?
- Where has silence become a strategy?

- Where has sarcasm become armor?

Activation

For the next week, practice one of these communication oils daily:

- Ask, *"What did you hear me say?"*
- Ask, *"What are you needing right now?"*
- Ask, *"Is this a good time for this conversation?"*
- Ask, *"Can I try that again more gently?"*

Do not measure success by agreement. Measure success by gentleness.

Prayer

Lord, teach us to speak so our words heal, to listen so our hearts understand, and to repair so our covenant remains whole. Seal the cracks where meaning has leaked. Guard us from assumption and fear. Restore the joy of being known. In Jesus' name, Amen.

Declaration (Spouse to Spouse)

I do not only love you; I pursue you. I do not only stay; I delight. I choose tenderness over tension, pursuit over passivity, and oil over dryness.

Affirmation (Personal)

My voice matters.

My longing is allowed.

My marriage is worth understanding.

***

When communication seals the leaks, marriage is no longer occupied with survival. It becomes free to build. Covenant was never designed merely to prevent collapse, but to produce fruit; to shape families, strengthen faith, and leave a legacy that outlives the couple who formed it.

***

CHAPTER 13

What Is a Drip-Free Marriage?

***

There was nothing remarkable about the afternoon, no anniversary celebration. No holiday. No conference. No ministerial gathering. No family milestone. It was simply Tuesday, and the house was quiet in the way homes become quiet when the children are grown, and the calendar has fewer demands than it once did. Andre sat in his chair near the window, reading glasses perched low on his nose, a light blanket over his legs. Keisha moved slowly in the kitchen, humming something soft while she rinsed a bowl and set it aside to dry. There was no rush to anything. The pace itself felt like prayer. From the outside, there was nothing dramatic to observe. No fiery romance. No urgent conflict resolution. No profound theological discourse. Just two aging bodies sharing space and time without friction. And yet, to those who knew their story, the moment was holy. What they had did not happen by accident. It had been built. It had been fought for. It had been repaired. It had been sealed. Visitors often remarked on how "peaceful" the home felt, as if peace were a personality trait instead of the product of years of forgiveness, tenderness, and small decisions to stay soft when life tempted them to become hard. When Andre reached for his tea, Keisha noticed his hand tremble slightly and walked over to steady the cup.

He did not protest. She did not explain. They simply moved as though their bodies had spent decades studying one another, and in many ways, they had.

Covenant in Old Age

Covenant looks unremarkable in old age to those who have not lived it. It looks like chairs are placed near enough to talk, but not so close that either feels crowded. It looks like knowing which days knees ache, which foods upset stomachs, and which memories should not be disturbed before noon. It looks like arguments that no longer require raised voices because the marriage has already survived louder storms. It looks like silence that is not emptiness but ease.

A drip-free marriage is not a marriage without storms; it is a marriage that remains standing after them.

When they first married, Andre assumed a good marriage was one that avoided conflict. Keisha assumed a good marriage was one that never lost romance. Both were wrong, but only time could teach them that. Marriage taught them instead that storms do not invalidate a covenant; storms reveal it.

Roofs are not evaluated on sunny days but on rainy ones. Love is not evaluated when life is simple, but when life is layered, compressed, and demanding. Only those who have weathered seasons can speak of covenant with tenderness instead of idealism. At their 40th anniversary dinner, their children asked for advice. Andre chuckled and said, "Just stay five minutes longer than your frustration." Keisha added, "And don't forget to apologize when you actually mean it." The table laughed, but beneath the humor was formation. Endurance is less about dramatic gestures and more about daily staying. There were years they stayed for the children, years they stayed for God, and eventually years they stayed because they liked one another again. All marriages have seasons where the "why" shifts. Covenant does not demand the same motive in every season; covenant holds while motives change.

The Power of Consistency

In their thirties, they endured financial scarcity. In their forties, they endured a health scare. In their fifties, they endured ministry disappointment. In their sixties, they endured the loss of both their parents. Each storm could have introduced leaks. Some did. But they learned to seal as they went. Sealants are applied when pressure is present, not after everything collapses.

To witness their marriage in old age was to witness resilience without spectacle. Nothing about them felt performative.

They did not post anniversary tributes on social media. They did not speak in marriage slogans. They did not correct younger couples with formulas. They simply embodied endurance. Embodiment is morc persuasive than instruction.

One afternoon, a young couple from their church came to visit. They sat at the same table where Andre and Keisha had once balanced checkbooks and argued about schedules and cried over disappointments. The young couple spoke about communication struggles, unmet expectations, and fear of drifting. Andre listened quietly, nodding in the slow, patient way of someone who no longer believes most problems require quick solutions.

Keisha offered tea and said, "Every marriage is allowed to be human before it becomes holy." The young couple didn't understand the sentence fully, but they would one day. Covenant does not make marriage easy; covenant makes marriage possible. Holiness does not erase humanity; it sanctifies it. A drip-free marriage is not flawless; it is sealed and sealed against assumption and sealed against bitterness. Sealed against contempt and sealed against the small leaks that destroy faster than the big storms.

As the young couple left, Keisha whispered, "They'll be alright. They're asking the right questions." Andre smiled, "And they like each other. Liking each other is half the battle." In younger years, they would have talked about love; in older years, they talked about like. Love was covenantal; like was choice, like required curiosity, humor, patience, and tenderness. Like was what made the marriage enjoyable after love had made it survivable.

The Beauty of a Drip-Free Marriage

Marriage in old age is marvelously unhurried. There is time to savor without rushing. There is time to remember without defending. There is time to apologize without shame. There is time to laugh without performing. And there is time to hold hands without any concern for who is watching. This is the beauty that young lovers do not yet know how to imagine.

When Keisha pulled the blanket up over Andre's knees, she did not think of herself as serving her husband. She thought of herself as tending to her friend. Friendship is the fruit of endurance. Romance is the blossom; friendship is the harvest. Blossoms are fragile. Harvest takes time.

A drip-free marriage becomes beautiful not because of what happens in the early years, but because of what remains in the latter ones.

What remains is what matters. Endurance in marriage is not merely the ability to stay married; it is the ability to remain tender. Many couples stay married but become cold. They live under the same roof but no longer share the same heart. They honor the covenant publicly but not privately.

They preserve the institution but lose the intimacy. A drip-free marriage outlives the moment because it outlives the temptation to become hardened.

Hardness is the great enemy of the covenant. Hardness does not appear suddenly; it accumulates over time through disappointment, fatigue, defensiveness, and fear. The heart becomes calloused from small cuts, the unreturned affection, the misunderstood comment, the unguarded sarcasm, the unresolved conflict. Keisha used to say, "We never broke; we just dried out." Dryness is more dangerous to marriage than a crisis. A crisis can wake a couple up. Dryness lulls them to sleep. A drip-free marriage learns to oil the heart in small ways, so the soul does not calcify.

Oil protects tenderness. Tenderness protects intimacy. Without tenderness, endurance becomes survival instead of beauty. Endurance also requires forgiveness. Forgiveness in marriage is less about grand confessions and more about the dozen small pardons offered each week. The quick apology for a sharp tone.

The gentle acknowledgment that a promise was forgotten. The willingness to let a bad mood pass without punishment. Forgiveness is not denial; forgiveness is maintenance. Maintenance prevents decay.

The Need for Small Acts of Reconnection

There was a season in their forties when Andre and Keisha were tempted to give up, not on marriage, but on enjoyment. They had endured conflict, rebuilt trust, rekindled intimacy, and repaired communication, but life was heavy. The Ministry required more than it returned. Their children demanded more than they could predict. Money arrived slowly and left quickly. Nights ended in exhaustion instead of pursuit. They were not angry; they were tired.

Most marriages do not end because of failure. They end because of fatigue. Fatigue makes everything feel expensive: conversation, affection, listening, prayer, and romance. When fatigue accumulates without oil, marriages shift from delight to duty. Duty can sustain marriage for a season, but it cannot produce fruit. Fruit requires joy. Joy requires margin. Margin requires intention. It was in those years that Andre and Keisha developed their practice of small Sabbaths. They would sit on the porch with coffee on Saturday mornings, say very little, and watch the neighborhood wake up. No agenda. No ministry planning.

No marriage talk. Just being. Being together is one of the most underrated practices of covenant. Performance is exhausting; being is restorative.

Being is also where friendship grows. Friendship in marriage is often confused with compatibility, but friendship is not compatibility; it is curiosity. Friendship asks questions, notices change, and delights in the other's existence. Compatibility asks, *"Do we fit?"* Friendship asks, "*Who are you today?*" Friendship makes marriage sustainable because bodies age, hormones shift, responsibilities multiply, and attraction evolves. Passion burns hot, but friendship burns long.

New Forms of Intimacy

In their fifties, Andre and Keisha discovered a new kind of intimacy, slower, gentler, and strangely more satisfying. Early marriage intimacy had been passionate and exploratory; mid-marriage intimacy had been logistical and negotiated; later intimacy became soulful. They no longer rushed through touch; they lingered. They no longer performed desire; they welcomed it. They no longer feared rejection; they trusted timing. This was not the intimacy taught in movies or preached from pulpits; this was the intimacy shaped by storms.

By their sixties, the mission began to emerge without being planned. Younger couples gravitated toward them without invitation. Not because they were outspoken about marriage, but because their marriage made people curious. Curiosity is a sign of witness. Witness is not about publicity; it is about visibility.

There is a quiet evangelism in a marriage that has survived storms without becoming bitter.

When the community held a marriage event one year ago, they were asked to share their story. Andre declined to speak from the podium and insisted their story did not need amplification. But during the reception afterward, three couples sat with them for hours, asking questions. "How did you rebuild trust?" "How did you handle seasons of dryness?" "How did you raise children without losing each other?" Andre and Keisha did not respond with formulas.

They responded with honesty. Honesty is more healing than advice. Keisha told one couple, "Trust doesn't return all at once; it returns in installments." *Andre added,* "And sometimes it comes on a different schedule than you expect." They both laughed, because this was truer than they had once known.

Resilience Through Disappointment

A drip-free marriage does not outlive the moment by avoiding disappointment.

It outlives the moment by metabolizing disappointment into wisdom. Wisdom is disappointment processed with tenderness. Many couples' experience disappointment; few couples transform it. Transformation is where resilience becomes testimony. Covenant also demands adaptability. The marriage you have at 25 is not the marriage you will have at 55. Bodies change. Desires change. Vocations change. Community changes. Children grow and leave. Health becomes fragile. Retirement demands renegotiation. Seasons shift whether couples prepare for them or not. A drip-free marriage learns to pivot without collapsing.

Keisha once told a friend, "Marriage is not one promise; it is a thousand promises disguised as one." She did not mean that vows were insufficient; she meant that vows must be renewed in micro-ways: in patience, in apology, in accommodation, in consideration, in affection, in silence, in listening, in staying. Vows are not protected by sentiment; vows are protected by repetition.

Drip-Free Marriage Defined

Endurance finally becomes beautiful when it is no longer driven by fear of failure but by delight in companionship. Not every couple reaches this stage. Some marriages end. Some repair and thrive. Some remain intact but emotionally distant. Some survive but resent. A drip-free marriage is not defined by perfection but by resilience that retains sweetness. Andre began walking with a cane in his seventies. Keisha slowed her steps to match his without comment. When she developed arthritis in her hands, Andre started opening jars and sealing envelopes before she asked.

This was not romance; this was devotion. *Devotion* is romance that has matured beyond performance. Early marriage offers butterflies; late marriage offers ballast. *Ballast* is what keeps the ship steady when storms return.

One evening, their granddaughter asked if they ever considered divorce. Andre chuckled, "Only during the first half." Keisha added, "By the second half, we were too invested to quit." They both smiled because they understood something she could not yet understand: investment makes covenant expensive, but it also makes covenant precious. *What costs nothing is rarely cherished. What is cherished is rarely abandoned.*

A drip-free marriage outlives the moment because it refuses to let fatigue become final. Fatigue is inevitable; finality is optional. Endurance is not carrying on without weakness; endurance is carrying on with weakness and without surrender. Weakness invites interdependence, and interdependence makes the covenant visible. *Witness* happens when private faithfulness becomes publicly observable without being publicly performed. No one sees vows whispered in a hospital room. No one sees forgiveness exchanged in the kitchen. No one sees the silent decision to apologize first. But those unseen acts accumulate into a reality that can be seen, an embodied testimony of covenant.

What younger couples admire in older couples is not the absence of pain but the absence of bitterness. *Bitterness* is pain without redemption; *tenderness* is pain redeemed. *Tenderness* is what makes marriage worth enduring. When a marriage reaches the stage where *tenderness* outlasts disappointment, the covenant becomes beautiful. And *beauty* is what makes the church interested again in marriage, not obligation, not doctrine, not fear, but *beauty*.

A drip-free marriage ultimately becomes future-shaped. It refuses to shrink the covenant down to the years of child-rearing or the decades of work or even the memories of youth. It thinks generationally, even if that generation is not biological.

Some couples bear children through wombs; others bear children through witness. Both are legitimate fruits. Both extend the covenant beyond the immediate moment.

Andre and Keisha did not talk about legacy much in their early years. Legacy seemed presumptuous. It felt like a conversation for wealthy families who passed down estates or for ministers with global platforms. But as they aged, they began to notice that their marriage was leaving a mark even without those trappings. Their children raised their own families with different temperaments but similar tenderness. Their grandchildren grew up with the certainty that love could last.

Couples in their church quietly watched how they spoke to one another, how they prayed, how they joked, how they disagreed, and how they recovered. Some legacies are inherited through DNA, others through discipleship. Legacy is the natural byproduct of endurance. When marriages endure with sweetness, they generate curiosity. Curiosity is the doorway to discipleship. We do not imitate what we begrudge; we imitate what we admire.

One afternoon, during a community meal, a young woman approached Keisha and said, "You make me believe marriage can still be good." She did not mean without conflict. She meant without cynicism. *Cynicism* is the slow rot of covenant.

Cynicism believes everything ends badly, so it stops investing in beauty. But *beauty* is what keeps covenant from becoming merely functional.

Endurance without beauty becomes stoicism. *Beauty* without endurance becomes fantasy. A drip-free marriage holds both.

When their church hosted a small marriage retreat, not with fanfare but with folding tables and crockpots, the facilitator did not ask Andre and Keisha to teach a seminar. He simply asked them to sit at one table and be available. Their presence was enough. That night, couples rotated through conversations with them like students at office hours, seeking not technique but testimony.

Testimony is a technique refined through storms. *Testimony* is also the language of Scripture. When the psalmists recount the faithfulness of God, they recount endurance. They speak of enemies conquered, valleys traversed, and mercies renewed. Covenant in Scripture is not static; it is storied. It unfolds across generations, across failures, across promises, and across waiting. Marriage, too, is storied. And stories are meant to be told, not hoarded. Andre and Keisha never imagined their story would matter to others. They simply assumed it mattered to them. But God uses what is witnessed, not merely what is experienced. Their marriage became a sermon without a pulpit.

The pulpit was the kitchen table, the porch swing, the hospital room, the church foyer, and the sanctuary aisle. Those who observed them did not hear doctrine; they saw covenant.

The question for every couple is not merely, "Will we stay married?" but "What will our marriage become?" Marriage can become a place of protection, a place of formation, a place of healing, a place of joy, a place of mission, or a place of resignation. A drip-free marriage becomes a place of pilgrimage, where two souls journey together toward holiness, not in perfection but in patience. Pilgrims do not walk quickly; they walk consistently. They rest. They drink. They sing. They suffer. They bless. They arrive. *Marriage is a pilgrimage.* Not every step is smooth, but every step matters.

The vision of a drip-free marriage must be spoken about because vision gives couples a target beyond crisis management. Most couples enter marriage imagining romance and companionship, not resilience. Resilience sounds too clinical, too cold, too mechanical. But resilience is simply love that has learned how to bend without breaking. Trees that survive storms do not survive because they are rigid, but because they are rooted and flexible. To build a marriage that outlives the moment, couples must aspire to three things: to endure, to enjoy, and to bless.

To endure means to stay when it is easier to leave, not at all costs, not in abuse, not in dehumanization, but in the ordinary trials of covenant.

Endurance is the courage to outlast fatigue, misunderstanding, and boredom.

To enjoy means to delight in the gift of one another. *Delight* cannot be manufactured under pressure; it must be cultivated in margin. Enjoyment is the fruit of friendship, humor, curiosity, and affection. Enjoyment is what keeps the covenant from being reduced to an assignment. To bless means to let your marriage overflow into the lives of others, not through perfection but through hospitality. When marriages bless, they send sons and daughters (biological or spiritual) into the world with less fear and more faith. A blessed marriage blesses.

Andre and Keisha's granddaughter once told them, "I want what you two have." She did not mean matching recliners or shared medical appointments. She meant a love that stayed. A love that did not wither when beauty faded. A love that did not drown when finances were tight. A love that did not shut down when communication was hard. A love that, without boasting, kept showing up.

When she asked for their secret, Andre laughed. "No secret. Just forgiveness." Keisha added, "And coffee. Lots of coffee." They laughed because there was truth in the simplicity. *Forgiveness and coffee* had accompanied them longer than any other practice. A drip-free marriage outlives the moment because it refuses to let the moment dictate the future. Moments are volatile; futures are cultivated. Moments are reactive; futures are intentional. Moments are felt; futures are formed. Marriage is not built in moments; it is built in practices. Practices create culture. Culture creates resilience. Resilience creates testimony. Testimony creates legacy.

Reflection

Consider carefully:

1. What storms have we survived?
2. What storms are we still weathering?
3. Where has fatigue tempted resignation?
4. Where has tenderness outlasted disappointment?
5. What has our marriage become?
6. What could our marriage yet become?

These are not questions of shame; they are invitations to vision.

Activation

This week, share your marriage story with someone younger or earlier in their journey—briefly, honestly, tenderly. Testimony honors endurance and multiplies faith. You did not endure only for yourselves.

Prayer

Lord, teach us to endure with tenderness. Restore laughter where dryness settled in. Turn fatigue into friendship, disappointment into wisdom,

and storms into testimony.

Seal our covenant against bitterness

and let our marriage become beautiful in old age.

In Jesus' name, Amen.

Declaration (Spouse to Spouse)

I choose to stay with tenderness, to repair with humility,

to endure with joy, and to finish with you.

Affirmation (Personal)

My marriage is not only for the moment. It is for the journey, the testimony, and the witness.

***

A drip-free marriage is not preserved by vision alone. What is built must be guarded. What is sealed must be tended. Covenant flourishes not in moments of inspiration but in rhythms of faithfulness.

***

Conclusion

Staying Leak-Proof

***

Marriage is not only built in the beginning; it is kept in the keeping. Many couples dream of the wedding, some dream of the baby years, a few dream of the retirement years, but very few dream of the daily maintenance that holds the house together when seasons shift and storms come. A drip-free marriage is not the result of a single vow spoken once at an altar, but of many smaller vows spoken in kitchens, cars, hospital rooms, counseling offices, and quiet bedrooms where no audience is present to applaud.

The older couples in their church always understood this intuitively. Weddings were events, but marriage was craftsmanship. No one expected a house to survive decades of summers and winters without attention; why would a marriage? There was a quiet dignity in the way those couples moved through life, repairing, repainting, replacing, and resealing. They did not brag about their longevity, but their consistency was its own testimony.

Young couples often asked them for their secret, and the secret was disappointingly ordinary: they paid attention.

They noticed when the other was weary. They asked questions when distance began to form. They reassured each other when insecurity flickered. They sealed their covenant not with spectacular gestures but with daily devotion. Over the years, devotion becomes architecture.

When couples first marry, they imagine love as a feeling, romance as a gesture, and commitment as a promise. Over time, they discover that love must also become a decision, romance must become a discipline, and commitment must become a practice. To stay leak-proof is to continue sealing what life inevitably tries to wear down.

In Chapter 13, we saw what a drip-free marriage becomes: a covenant that endures with tenderness. But endurance alone is not enough. Endurance must be supported by maintenance, and maintenance must be practiced long after the crisis has passed. It is easier to fix a leak when water is pouring into the room than it is to maintain the roof in clear weather. Many couples survive the storm, only to neglect the season that follows it. A marriage that endures deserves to be maintained. To stay leak-proof requires humility. Humility admits that no marriage graduates from maintenance.

Couples do not age out of needing affection, conversation, forgiveness, or curiosity. They do not become so seasoned that they no longer require apology.

They do not become so mature that they no longer require intentionality. The marriages that inspire are not the marriages that have outgrown the basic disciplines, but the ones that have returned to them again and again without embarrassment. Humility also acknowledges weakness without shame. Every spouse has places where they drip: irritabilities, disappointments, fears, insecurities, habits, histories, and unhealed places. Marriage does not replace sanctification; it exposes the places that require it. Keisha once confessed to a friend that marriage did not make her holy; marriage made her aware. Awareness is not condemnation; it is an invitation. An invitation is where marriage becomes beautiful. To invite a spouse into one's weakness is to open a window for love to seal what pride cannot. Pride hides leaks; humility names them. Anything hidden in marriage eventually becomes mold. The sooner leaks are exposed to light; the sooner repair can begin.

The Practices of Maintenance: Inspection, Oiling, Sealing

Staying leak-proof also involves tending to the small seals that prevent larger ruptures. Seasonal maintenance often involves three practices: inspection, oiling, and sealing.

Inspection in marriage is not interrogation; it is curiosity. Curiosity asks, "How are we really doing?" without assuming it already knows the answer. Curiosity listens without preparing a defense.

Curiosity refuses to believe that marriage can be understood without regular updates. People change. Seasons change. Emotional weather shifts. Curiosity prevents marriage from becoming outdated in its knowledge of the other.

Oiling is the daily application of tenderness, the soft touches, the inside jokes, the shared meals, the intentional affirmations, the small gifts, the smiles across rooms, the way a spouse's name sounds when spoken warmly. Oil prevents friction from becoming injury. Oil prevents fatigue from becoming resentment. Oil keeps desire from drying out when life is demanding.

Sealing is the practice of closure. Closure prevents open loops from becoming bitterness. Closure does not demand that every disagreement conclude with perfect agreement; it requires that disagreements not remain indefinitely open. Unsealed conflicts become drafts that chill the home over time. Sealing involves apology, clarification, forgiveness, understanding, and sometimes compromise. Couples who seal well rarely accumulate resentment.

It is common for couples to overestimate the value of grand gestures and underestimate the value of maintenance.

Grand gestures make memories. Maintenance makes marriages. Grand gestures can be posted online. Maintenance is witnessed only by God and the one you promised to love.

To stay leak-proof, couples must remain attentive to the ordinary. Ordinary faithfulness is the unsung hero of the covenant. Ordinary faithfulness prepares meals, attends appointments, pays bills, prays quietly, shows up to events, listens to stories already told, and remains consistent even when uncelebrated. Ordinary faithfulness is the backbone of extraordinary marriages.

Remaining leak-proof also includes the willingness to repair. **Repair** is not an admission of failure; it is an admission of value. People repair what they treasure. A marriage that never repairs is a marriage that has ceased to matter. Repair involves noticing when tone has grown sharp, when sarcasm has become armor, when silence has become punishment, when avoidance has become habit, when intimacy has become rare, and when respect has become optional. Couples who repair do not wait for a crisis to justify action.

Guarding the Thresholds

Sealing leaks also requires managing what enters the home. In ancient times, houses were built with thresholds because thresholds-controlled access. Marriages, too, need thresholds.

Thresholds guard against comparison, emotional entanglements, isolation, contempt, spiritual dryness, and distractions that erode affection. Couples do not stay leak-proof by accident; they stay leak-proof by learning to guard the doors of the home together.

The Spiritual Component of Maintenance

There is also a spiritual component to staying leak-proof. Scripture describes a covenant as something God seals, sustains, and sanctifies. Covenants require grace because covenants demand more than human strength can produce consistently. Grace does not exempt couples from effort; grace empowers them for it. Without grace, marriage becomes self-reliance; with grace, marriage becomes mutual reliance on the One who sustains the covenant. Grace allows spouses to confess weakness without being discarded. Grace allows conflict to mature without destroying intimacy. Grace allows desire to be reborn after disappointment. Grace allows history to become testimony. Testimony is what makes marriage worth sharing.

Rhythm and Prayer

Staying leak-proof requires rhythm. Rhythm establishes predictability, and predictability establishes safety. Couples who have rhythms of prayer, rhythms of communication, rhythms of affection, rhythms of

Sabbath, rhythms of laughter, and rhythms of service rarely leak without noticing. The rhythms become detection systems long before leakage becomes damage.

Finally, staying leak-proof involves remembering. Marriage has a memory. Memories of how love started, how storms were survived, how intimacy was restored, how forgiveness was exchanged, how laughter returned, how Jesus was invited, how counsel was received, how covenants were held. Memory is the anchor that prevents temporary frustration from erasing permanent affection. Couples who remember well rarely resign easily.

A roof is tested by rain, but it is preserved by maintenance. Storms test a marriage, but it is preserved by tenderness. Storms reveal quality; maintenance reveals devotion. Devotion is what turns marriage from a contract into a covenant.

Andre and Keisha did not become leak-proof overnight. There were seasons when the roof groaned under the pressure of weather they did not expect. There were leaks they ignored because naming them felt embarrassing.

Some storms forced them to rearrange the furniture of their souls. But somewhere along the journey, not at the beginning, not even in the middle, but in the long stretch between raising children and becoming grandparents, they began to see the fruit of maintenance.

It did not happen with fanfare. No one applauded. No anniversary speech captured it. It was simply the quiet relief of a home that no longer let water through.

They still disagreed. They still got tired. They still misunderstood one another at times. But the leaks no longer threatened the foundation. Marriage had become shelter, not exposure.

From the beginning, Scripture frames marriage as shelter. In Genesis, God observes that "it is not good for the man to be alone," and responds not with pity but with covenantal companionship (Gen. 2:18). Before there was church or city, there was marriage. Before there were ceremonies or contracts, there was union. And before there were children or culture, there was covering. The first covenant God formed between humans was not economic or political, but relational. Marriage was designed to answer loneliness with belonging and to answer vulnerability with refuge.

Legacy of a Drip-Free Marriage

Late in their seventies, they hosted a small gathering at their home. Nothing fancy, just folding chairs, iced tea, and finger foods. The invitation list was short: a few couples from church, two young pastors they had mentored, and a newly married pair who arrived still carrying the afterglow of their wedding photos.

Someone asked Andre and Keisha to share their best marriage advice. Andre shook his head. "I don't know about advice," he said, "but I can tell you what helped us stay." Keisha smiled and said, "And that is advice."

The younger couples leaned in, not because they expected to hear philosophy, but because they hoped to hear something they could actually do. One of the newly married wives admitted she feared waking up one day next to a stranger. Keisha smiled gently. "Then don’t stop learning from each other," she said. "People change. Even the person you love will become someone new over time. The goal isn’t to freeze who they were, it’s to stay curious about who they are becoming." There was laughter around the room, but there was also relief. Curiosity, it seemed, was not only for courtship. It was for a covenant.

They did not speak about secrets, formulas, or techniques. They spoke about maintenance. They spoke about forgiveness as if it were a daily discipline, not an event.

They spoke about laughter as oil, softness as shield, and prayer as oxygen. They spoke about touch not as an obligatory marital duty but as a language that kept the heart fluent. They spoke about humility not as humiliation but as courage. They spoke about the long obedience of the covenant.

One of the younger husbands asked them how they knew they would make it. Keisha answered, "We didn't." She took Andre's hand. "We just refused to stop trying to seal what was leaking." That sentence carried more weight than any seminar outline could deliver. Trying, in the context of covenant, is not desperation; it is devotion. Trying is how marriages stay leak-proof.

What made their marriage compelling was not that they avoided storms, but that storms no longer defined them. In their early years, storms were announcements, loud, disruptive, disorienting. In their later years, storms were simply weather. They prepared, they covered, they waited, they prayed, and they continued. Their marriage had become shelter, not spectacle.

A young bride at the gathering asked, "But what about when the damage has already happened?"

Keisha nodded gently. "Houses can be repaired," she said. "So can marriages. But you must decide the house is worth keeping."

The room grew quiet because everyone knew she was not talking about drywall. She was talking about dignity.

The book of Proverbs says, *"By wisdom a house is built, and through understanding it is established; through knowledge its rooms are filled with rare and beautiful treasures"* (Prov. 24:3–4, NIV).

Proverbs does not describe marriage as something sustained by passion or sentiment alone. It uses the language of building, establishing, and filling. Wisdom builds the frame. Understanding stabilizes the structure. Knowledge furnishes the rooms with *"rare and beautiful treasures."* This is the architecture of the covenant.

No storm, however fierce, can dismantle a house built with wisdom, stabilized by understanding, and filled with knowledge. Romance may ignite a marriage, but wisdom is what keeps it from collapsing. Wisdom builds, understanding stabilizes, and knowledge decorates. Many couples try to decorate without stabilizing or stabilize without building. The order matters. Rare and beautiful treasures are enjoyed only in homes that have been properly established.

Near the end of the evening, someone asked how they stayed in love for so long. Andre chuckled. "We didn't stay in love," he said. "We loved, and the love stayed." Keisha squeezed his arm. "And when it didn't stay, we went and got it back." Love that stays is not passive. It is retrieved, carried, restored, forgiven, and maintained.

The prophet Malachi asks a question that sounds almost out of place until you read it slowly: *"Has not the Lord made them one?"* Then, almost as if anticipating our curiosity, he adds, *"And why one? Because He was seeking godly offspring"* (Mal. 2:15). Offspring there is not limited to biology; it includes witness, discipleship, culture, and legacy. A godly legacy is not produced merely through wombs but through homes. A marriage that becomes shelter produces fruit that extends beyond the couple themselves. Children, grandchildren, parishioners, friends, and onlookers all eat from the tree of a covenant that has weathered storms.

Years later, at their 60th anniversary celebration, their oldest grandson stood to make a toast. He was not eloquent, but he was sincere. "Grandma and Grandpa's marriage was like a roof that held," he said. "We grew up underneath it. We never worried about rain." There were misty eyes around the room because many in attendance remembered homes where the roof did not hold, where storms came through the ceiling and drenched childhood.

To grow up under a roof that holds is to grow up with the confidence that love can endure without breaking.

After the toast, their granddaughter added something none of them expected. "Grandma and Grandpa's house didn't just keep the rain out," she said. "It kept the fear out. We felt safe here."

There was a hush because safety is a rare inheritance. Many grow up learning to brace themselves for the next outburst, the next disappointment, the next silent treatment, the next slammed door.

But their grandchildren had learned something else entirely: how to exhale. Safety, once experienced in childhood, becomes the blueprint for intimacy in adulthood.

To give a child safety is to give them something they will spend the rest of their lives trying to recreate with the person they love.

A drip-free marriage becomes a witness. It preaches without a pulpit, teaches without a curriculum, and testifies without a microphone. It answers cultural cynicism with demonstration, not debate. It reveals that the covenant is not archaic or oppressive but liberating in a way only safety can liberate. When marriages become safe, souls have room to flourish.

The Psalms repeatedly describe God as shelter: *"a refuge from the storm," "a strong tower," "a hiding place,"* and *"a dwelling of safety."* These images are not accidental. Shelter is the language of covenant. When a marriage becomes shelter, it participates in the same imagery Scripture uses to describe God's faithfulness. A home that keeps out the storm becomes a parable for all who enter it. Not every visitor can articulate the theology, but they can feel the safety. Some of the most profound sermons are preached through houses that hold.

Not every couple will have children or grandchildren beneath their roof, but every marriage has the capacity to shelter someone. Some marriages shelter nieces and nephews. Some shelter spiritual sons and daughters. Some shelter friends, congregants, neighbors, or weary leaders. Some shelters can protect entire communities simply by refusing to collapse.

The legacy a marriage leaves is not measured by how impressive it appears from a distance, but by how many people find shade beneath it. Beauty and resilience are evangelistic. People gravitate toward marriages that hold. They do not have to be perfect; they simply have to remain.

Staying leak-proof is not only about survival, but also about witness. When the roof holds, the house becomes more than a house. It becomes a refuge.

The apostle Paul calls marriage *"a profound mystery"* (Eph. 5:32). Mystery does not mean confusion; it means revelation. A mystery is something that must be witnessed before it is understood. Marriage reveals covenant, imperfectly, humbly, and through much forgiveness, but it reveals nonetheless. When a marriage becomes refuge, it reveals something about the God who covers, restores, and holds. When a marriage becomes witness, it reveals something about the God who keeps promises. Covenant is not a metaphor for marriage; marriage is a metaphor for covenant.

Reflection

Consider carefully:

1. Where has our marriage leaked in the past, and how did we respond?
2. What storms have we survived that deserve to be remembered?
3. What do we need to maintain now so we are not repairing later?
4. What rhythms keep our marriage tender and leak-proof?
5. Who has grown under the shade of our covenant?
6. Who might God allow to find shelter under our roof in the years to come?

Reflection does not shame – it clarifies.

Clarity is one of the great gifts a marriage can receive.

Activation

This week, share your marriage story with someone younger or earlier in their journey; briefly, honestly, tenderly. Testimony honors endurance and multiplies faith. You did not endure only for yourselves.

Prayer

Lord, seal our marriage where life has worn the edges thin. Oil our speech so tenderness returns.

Guard our threshold from what corrodes love and dries out affection. Give us humility to repair and courage to forgive.

Let our home be a shelter, not a battlefield; a place of laughter, not contempt; a place of blessing, not withdrawal. Teach us again how to enjoy one another.

Teach us again how to endure with beauty. And let the storms that find a roof that holds. In Jesus' name, Amen.

Declaration

***

I choose you, not only in memory, but in this season and the seasons ahead. I will repair with humility. I will seal with tenderness, I will bless with intention, and I will stay with joy.

Affirmation

Our marriage is not finished. We are still becoming.

And by God's grace, we will remain.

Affirmation

We speak life over our marriage. We choose repair over retreat.

We choose tenderness over withdrawal. We choose forgiveness over scorekeeping.

We seal the leaks that threaten our covenant.

We tend to the cracks that form beneath busyness.

We refuse the slow erosion of neglect. We resist the quiet drip of contempt.

We honor one another in word and in touch. We protect desire from shame and secrecy. We nurture intimacy as a gift, not a burden.

We guard our home from comparison and distraction.

We pursue laughter. We pursue affection. We pursue peace.

We pursue connection.

We acknowledge that storms will come, but we will not surrender our shelter.

We will not abandon our vow.

We will not treat our covenant as disposable.

We welcome the work of maintenance. We welcome the work of restoration. We welcome the work of healing.

We welcome God into the house we are building.

By grace, we become leak-proof. By wisdom, we become established.

By love, we become a refuge for others.

In unity, we prosper. In covenant, we endure.

Benediction

* * *

May your marriage become a shelter. May storms come, but not consume.

May the roof hold.

May the walls remain steady.

May the covenant stand through wind and rain.

May laughter return to the rooms. May affection soften the hallways.

May forgiveness lift the ceilings once again.

May small leaks be noticed early.

May great leaks be repaired with grace. May bitterness find no corner to hide in.

May contempt find no doorway through which to enter.

May desire flow without shame. May tenderness flow without fear.

May intimacy be tended like a garden and enjoyed like a well of living water.

May your home become a witness.

May children grow beneath its shade. May our neighbors rest in its testimony. May generations bless its memory.

And when the rain comes, and it will,

may you discover that God Himself has become your sealant, your shelter,

your covering, and your peace.

In the name of the Father, and of the Son, and of the Holy Spirit. Amen.

Drip-Free Marriage Discussion & Reflection Guide

***

How to Use This Guide

This guide is designed for couples, small groups, and marriage cohorts who want to move from inspiration to intentional practice. It may be used privately between spouses or within a structured group setting.

Each chapter includes four movements:

Clarify — What did we learn?
Reveal — What does this expose in us?
Practice — What will we apply?
Pray — How will we invite God into this area?

Take your time. Honest conversation matters more than quick completion.

SECTION I

The Problem of the Drip

Chapter 1

Your Marriage Is One of a Kind

Clarify

What makes our marriage story unique?

What strengths define us that we may overlook?

Reveal

Where have we compared our marriage to others? How has comparison shaped our expectations?

Practice

Name one strength in your marriage that you will intentionally protect this month. Speak one specific affirmation to your spouse about their contribution to your story.

Pray

Ask God to guard the uniqueness of your covenant and remove comparison from your perspective.

Chapter 2

The Dripping Marriage

Clarify

What small "drips" were described in this chapter?

Which ones feel familiar?

Reveal

What patterns of neglect or tone have we normalized?

What issue have we dismissed as small that may be cumulative?

Practice

Choose one recurring tension and address it calmly this week. Replace one negative pattern with a specific positive action.

Pray

Invite wisdom to recognize leaks early and humility to repair them quickly.

Chapter 3

A Marriage "Porn Apart"

Clarify

How does cultural fantasy distort marital expectations?

What messages about sex shaped us before marriage?

Reveal

Where have unrealistic comparisons affected intimacy?

Where has silence replaced honesty?

Practice

Commit to one boundary that protects intimacy. Schedule a calm, honest conversation about expectations.

Pray

Ask God to renew your understanding of covenant intimacy.

Chapter 4

Rooftop Living: When Couples Retreat Instead of Connect

Clarify

What does emotional retreat look like?

How can busyness disguise withdrawal?

Reveal

Where have we avoided repair?

What conversation have we postponed?

Practice

Initiate one difficult but necessary conversation.

Set aside one protected time for undistracted connection this week.

Pray

Ask for courage to pursue connection rather than retreat.

SECTION II

The Oils and Sealants That Keep Love Alive

Chapter 5

What a Man Wants / What a Woman Wants

Clarify

What core longings were described for husbands and wives? Which resonated most deeply with you?

Reveal

Where have I loved from preference rather than understanding? Where have I assumed instead of asking?

Practice

Complete this sentence for your spouse:

"I feel most respected when…"

"I feel most cherished when…"

Apply one insight this week.

Pray

Ask for understanding that translates lovc accuratcly.

Chapter 6

Marriage Spices

Clarify

What makes marriage flavorful rather than predictable? What elements reintroduce delight?

Reveal

Has routine replaced intentionality?

Where have we stopped pursuing one another?

Practice

Plan one intentional gesture this week.

Reintroduce playfulness into one shared moment.

Pray

Invite joy back into everyday interactions.

Chapter 7

Redeeming Sexual Formation

Clarify

What shaped your sexual understanding before marriage?

How did church, family, or culture influence you?

Reveal

Where does shame still influence intimacy?

What fears remain unspoken?

Practice

Share one formative experience with your spouse.

Replace one distorted belief with redemptive truth.

Pray

Ask God to heal what formed desire incorrectly.

Chapter 8

SucSEXful Marriage: From Prohibition to Passion

Clarify

How does covenant make pleasure safe?

What distinguishes mutual passion from sclfish pursuit?

Reveal

Have we approached intimacy from fear or celebration?

Where has mutual attentiveness weakened?

Practice

Discuss what makes intimacy meaningful beyond performance. Practice attentiveness rather than assumption.

Pray

Thank God for desire as a sacred gift within covenant.

Chapter 9

SOS: Save Our Sex

Clarify

What causes intimacy to cool over time?

What warning signs were described?

Reveal

Are we avoiding necessary repair conversations?

Where has resentment entered the bedroom?

Practice

Schedule a repair conversation.

Be intentional rather than waiting for spontaneity.

Pray

Ask for restoration where distance has formed.

Chapter 10

The Power of Touch

Clarify

Why is non-sexual touch foundational?

How does tenderness sustain connection?

Reveal

Have we reduced touch only to initiation?

Where has everyday affection faded?

Practice

Introduce daily affectionate touch with no agenda.

Hold one extended embrace each day this week.

Pray

Invite gentleness into your physical connection.

Chapter 11

Re-Oiling the Marriage

Clarify

What does maintenance look like in covenant?

Why does friction increase without renewal?

Reveal

Where are we running dry?

What rhythms need restoration?

Practice

Create one weekly marriage ritual.

Review shared goals monthly.

Pray

Ask for faithfulness in consistent small habits.

Chapter 12

Communication: The Sealant Against Leaks

Clarify

How does misinterpretation create conflict?

What role does tone play in tension?

Reveal

What assumptions have I made recently?

Where have I reacted instead of clarifying?

Practice

Use this sentence: "Help me understand what you meant."

Pause before responding when emotionally activated.

Pray

Invite wisdom into every conversation.

SECTION III

The Vision of a Leak-Proof Covenant

Chapter 13

What Is a Drip-Free Marriage?

Clarify

How is a drip-free marriage defined?

What fruit should covenant produce?

Reveal

Are we surviving or building?

What legacy are we shaping?

Practice

Write a one-paragraph vision statement for your marriage. Identify one value you want to pass on generationally.

Pray

Ask God to make your marriage fruitful and enduring.

Conclusion

Staying Leak-Proof

Clarify

What sustains long-term health?

Why is vigilance necessary?

Reveal

Where are we vulnerable to future erosion?

What patterns must remain guarded?

Practice

Schedule quarterly covenant check-ins.

Commit to immediate repair rather than delayed response.

Pray

Ask for endurance, humility, and joy in the long journey.

Continue the Drip-Free Journey

Marriage strengthens through intentional growth.

Scan below to access the *30-Day Drip-Free Challenge*, additional resources, and coaching tools designed to help you build, maintain, and protect your covenant.

Acknowledgments

***

No marriage is built alone, and no book about marriage is written in isolation.

First and foremost, I give thanks to God, the Author of covenant and the Sustainer of love. Whatever wisdom these pages carry has been shaped by His grace, refined through prayer, and sharpened through seasons of both clarity and stretching. If this book brings healing to any home, the glory belongs to Him.

To my wife, thank you for walking this journey of covenant with strength, intelligence, humor, and grace. You have not only shared life with me; you have helped me understand it more deeply. Your partnership has sharpened my thinking, softened my edges, and strengthened my faith. Writing about marriage while living it is no small task, and I am grateful that our life together continues to be a place of learning and joy.

To my parents, whose forty years of marriage modeled endurance, loyalty, and devotion, your legacy continues to instruct me. The way you honored covenant shaped how I understand commitment. Even in your absence, your example remains present.

To the countless couples I have had the privilege of counseling, teaching, and walking alongside, thank you. Your questions, honesty, struggles, and courage to grow have informed these pages more than you know. While confidentiality prevents me from naming you, your stories echo throughout this work. This book exists because real couples were willing to do *real work.*

To mentors, pastors, and leaders who have spoken into my life over the years, your counsel, correction, and encouragement have strengthened both my ministry and my marriage. Leadership is never solitary, and I am grateful for those who invested in me long before this manuscript existed.

To the churches and communities that create space for honest conversations about marriage, thank you for refusing silence where healing is needed. Strong marriages build strong families, and strong families build enduring communities.

And finally, to every reader who has chosen to lean into this work rather than drift, thank you. Marriage requires humility, courage, and consistency. The fact that you are willing to examine, repair, and strengthen your covenant is already a sign of hope.

May your home be sealed against erosion. May your love grow wiser with time.

And may your covenant become shelter for generations.

In God, we are sealed.

About the Author

***

Dr. Elsworth Neale is a family life educator, pastor, researcher, and relationship coach with over two decades of experience serving individuals, couples, and families. He is widely respected for his integrative approach to faith, psychology, and relational formation.

With more than twenty years of teaching, counseling, and leadership experience, Dr. Neale integrates biblical conviction, relational science, and lived wisdom to help couples build resilient, intentional covenants. His work focuses on identifying relational patterns, repairing emotional erosion, and equipping marriages to endure with clarity and purpose.

He believes strong marriages are not accidental; they are cultivated through understanding, discipline, and grace. He and his wife continue the daily work of covenant, committed to building a love that strengthens with time and endures with wisdom and grace.

www.ingramcontent.com/pod-product-compliance
Lightning Source LLC
LaVergne TN
LVHW090551110826
845146LV00001B/100